In-Tuition
Moments of Awakening

Joanna Infeld

KO
RA

KORA
PRESS

This book is dedicated to all those who search for the truth, and are endeavoring to share their discoveries with others.

From the Publisher

Kora Press is proud to present *In-Tuition; Moments of Awakening* by Joanna Infeld, previously published in Canada and now re-edited and enlarged. This is another in a series of publications dedicated to human development, the search for truth and the human story. In this book the usher, or teacher is a master who instructs within a mysterious school that can only be accessed by those who are desperately seeking for answers to questions concerning the reasons for living and for their unique part within this earthly journey.

The main character of the book is a young woman who, disillusioned with her marriage and her mundane life, undertakes a search for knowledge and the truth. To her surprise, she finds what she is looking for but her quest leads her to more questions than answers. A real journey into the mystery of life is like that: it will produce a further hunger to find out more...

This book is part of a trilogy. The other two parts (a prequel and a sequel) are currently in preparation.

If you enjoy *In-Tuition; Moments of Awakening,* perhaps you will be interested in other books by the same author from Kora Press:

Rainbow Woman
Unmasked; Spirit Flares

A little ant was traversing a large imprint of a foot in the sand. As it reached the other side, it thought to itself, "Phew, that was a great canyon."

Contents

Foreword

Foreword

It might appear that more than two weeks pass from the beginning of this story till its end, especially if you take into account the many encounters, mornings, afternoons and evenings. However, this is not so, for the time spent at the Human Development Center is fairy time, wherein many days or even years can pass, whereas the time elapsed in the human world is much shorter, sometimes even equal to only a few hours or days.

We measure time according to our own perceptions and limitations, governed primarily by the movement of the sun, the moon and the stars. Time elsewhere (elsewhere in the universe or even elsewhere right here) takes on totally different qualities and significances and cannot be measured by a mechanical device at all.

Part One

How It All Began

Chapter One
The Discovery

Ireally didn't mean to know. I wished I could reverse the onslaught of time and be ignorant again. I have no idea what caused me to put my hand into his jacket pocket as I took his suit to the cleaners. I never look through his pockets; it's the kind of thing you read about in novels, but if two people trust each other, you don't need to... Who am I kidding? I would so much like to think of myself as a sophisticated wife, secure and happy, trusting and loving. But suddenly all that wishful thinking was shattered in one brief moment as I stood in front of the counter and the lady asked me whether I wanted to check the pockets before I left the suit to be cleaned. It wasn't even my idea, as if the whole thing was a terrible joke played out by fate and everyone else, while I remained like a puppet, whose strings were being pulled by some invisible hands.

So there I was, jacket in one hand and that dreaded hotel bill in the other—I must have been quite a sight, seeing my name on a bill —Mr. and Mrs. Johnson—for a room at a place I had never been to. My mind was racing—September sixth, what day of the week was that? I couldn't think. I put the jacket back on the counter, took the receipt, even managed a smile and a "thank you" and dashed out of the door. I almost ran to the car, let myself in, threw my bag onto the passenger's seat and sat there, slowly gathering my thoughts, resting the bill in front of my eyes, using the steering wheel as a pulpit.

I didn't want to know on the one hand and I could have easily torn up the offending piece of paper and thrown it out of the window, pretending that this was not really happening. But there was also a great curiosity to know more. Who is she? Where did they go? What was the name of that hotel? were questions that were rattling around in my head, demanding answers. I carefully scrutinized the bill— The Golden Dusk Hotel. Hotel. Never heard of it. Certainly not a major chain or group of hotels. In a way that was a relief; it wasn't somewhere where we had been together, say for dinner or afternoon tea. And even as I looked, I was playing out scenarios in my head: The Confrontation and The Questioning. This was a drama with tragic-comic undertones with the final result being separation and divorce. Then there was the Playing Ignorance spy-thriller, trying to find out more, hiding around corners, opening letters, searching drawers and pockets for more evidence.

Mr. and Mrs. Johnson at the Golden Dusk Hotel—one night, breakfast and two phone calls. Even the phone numbers were on the bill. One was our home—he had phoned home—and one was to the office. Both numbers were so familiar to me, probably etched in my memory forever. The date—September sixth. When was that? I couldn't think; it was more than six weeks ago. It couldn't have been a weekend; I could account for every one of them. My mind was racing. I had a small diary in my bag—I pulled it out. Dentist appointment—that was the first thing I noticed about Tuesday, September sixth. Then, in small letters it said underneath: Andrew away at conference. The same writing appeared within the box for the previous Sunday and Monday as well. A three-day conference. He was away for three days. That's right! I remembered now. I sighed and leaned back in the seat, as floods of memories from those three days rushed in. I could clearly see little snapshots of life at home, the things I did during those three days. And then I pictured the faces of his colleagues, the ones that I knew, who were supposed to have gone too. And then the one thing I did not want to submit to came in as an avalanche of doubt and suspicion: Who was he with? Who could it be? In my mind's eye I searched a gallery of portraits—faces of friends, people we knew, people we met. Women, friends, colleagues. It was useless; I didn't know. It could be anybody; it shouldn't be anybody. Who knows how a man thinks? Sitting here is not going to solve anything. I needed to think this through. I needed to talk to somebody. I needed time.

I started the car and slowly drove towards home. I took my time as I tried to gather my thoughts. There were so many things I wanted to do—I wanted to run away, to confront him, to hire a detective to follow him and then I wanted to forget all those ideas and do nothing at all, to pretend nothing was happening so that life could carry on as before. But, of course, I knew it couldn't. I knew it never would be the same again.

When I got home, the house felt empty. I paced around the place, checking messages, making myself a cup of tea. I couldn't sit still, I didn't know what to do. As always, when at loss, I dialed Anne's familiar number. She was home. She answered the phone. Now what do I say? She picked up that something was wrong. After all, we knew each other well.

"Are you all right?" she asked.

Tears flooded to my eyes, as I answered, "No, I'm not. Can I come over?"

She always liked a good drama. "Sure," she said, "come right away."

On my way over to Anne's house I became subject to two mental processes, both related to and dependent on each other. The first was a great value and appreciation for the normality of things, and a further longing for life to be boring, mundane, uneventful, continuous and secure. I also felt the beginning of a realization that all that had now changed and that nothing would be the same ever again. I couldn't even begin to think about the future, for my whole life, as I knew it, stood in front of me in ruins now and I had no idea how to go about repairing it.

Then, in my desperate quest for some sort of solace or comfort, I found my mind racing through the various books I had read and films I had seen, in search of a similar scenario. I was sure this was a stereotype situation, very banal and a veritable template for many cheap paperback stories, which I used to consume voraciously when I was a teenager. And yet, for the life of me, I couldn't remember what ought to happen next according to any one of them. And then, suddenly, I remembered and it almost caused me to stop the car in the middle of the traffic. Of course, the wife doesn't find out till later, but it is always her best friend who is having an affair with her husband! Of course, Anne! How could I have not spotted it before? I'm going over to her place to pour my heart out and she will be mocking me because she already knows all about it. No doubt she will then urge me to get a divorce so she can have him all to herself! I quickly scanned in my mind all the times we had been out together, the three of us, and how well Anne and Andrew used to get on, how pleased I was and relieved that both of my favorite people enjoyed each other's company. What a fool I had been.

And then a further thought came into my head and that was that perhaps the hotel bill was left in his pocket on purpose, so that I would find it, demand an explanation and file for a divorce. Perhaps it was part of a plan, all thought out and premeditated to place the ball in my court, for me to make the decisions. Perhaps not completely consciously, but as part of a plan nevertheless.

In the meantime, I was nearing Anne's home and I needed to decide what I was going to tell her, how I would be with her and what would I give her the satisfaction of hearing. Before I had time to really think about it, I was parked outside her house and before I even had time to lock up the car, she was standing in the doorway waiting for me to reach her at the top of the porch steps. As I walked toward her, I could see that she knew right away that something was the matter—she knew me too well. There was no point in pretending any more. I didn't want to anyway; I needed to talk to someone. And if it was her, then she would need to deal with her own guilt and decide whether she would be honest with me or not. I didn't care any more. It needed to come out into the open.

Anne put the kettle on to make tea, as she always did when I visited her. As soon as we sat down together in her living room, she asked, "What is the matter?"

I immediately blurted out, to my own surprise as well as hers, "Andrew is having an affair!"

"Really?" she sounded genuinely surprised, but not shocked, and the next thing she asked was, "How do you know?"

So before I knew it, I was telling her the whole story, which wasn't much of a story, really, for all there was to report was the discovery at the dry cleaner's and that's it, with a few more speculations, indignations, surprises and bewilderments on my part. She seemed very sympathetic and quiet, with a few questions that I had already thought about, like, "When looking back, isn't there anything else you can see that now seems suspicious? Like unexpected business trips or unexplained expenses?"

Well, sure there was, but that's the way Andrew was anyway and that was the nature of his job—traveling a lot, spending generously during his trips and then claiming back expenses—it was all very difficult to keep track of. Money in, money out. I always saw myself as the policeman standing in the middle of a busy crossroads, directing the traffic, but never holding on to much in the process and never really investigating where the traffic was coming from or where it was going. As long as it was there, I had places to send it; as long as I could pay the bills and the mortgage for the next month, I trusted that the next bit would come in somehow so that we could continue. And so far it always did.

"Nothing more unexpected than usual," I replied, thinking hard, but not able to relate to anything suspicious or out of the ordinary, like an exotic perfume or unfamiliar scent.

"What about the classic one, lipstick on his collar?" Anne said, pouring another cup of tea. I couldn't control it and despite my grief and confusion, I burst out laughing.

"Oh, please," I said, indignant, though I knew I had no right to be after what had happened so far. "He would never do that."

"That's what every wife in your situation always says. But it does happen because it's one way of letting you know," Anne said, now turning into a psychologist. I could almost see her in a white coat with a pad and pencil in her hand. "Another, of course, is to leave a hotel bill in his coat pocket."

This thought took me by surprise. Not because I hadn't thought of that already, but because I didn't expect her to come up with it. I pretended to be ignorant or naïve or both.

"Are you saying that he did it deliberately?"

"Well, not necessarily consciously or deliberately," Anne explained, obviously pleased that I was taking her seriously. "But something in him wanted you to know, otherwise he would not have left that bill there. I believe," she added, with an air of authority, "that if someone wants to do something but doesn't know how and hesitates for too long, then their sub-conscious mind will find the opportunity to do it on its terms, whether the person agrees to those terms or not."

"Oh, Anne, you mean he wanted me to know so that I would take the initiative and walk away from our relationship? Or perhaps decide that I can forgive him and carry on? Is it that he can no longer live with the lie and the guilt?" I did not wait for an answer to all these questions that were spilling out, one after the other. "So what should I do? What would you do in my situation?" I asked rather pathetically, putting myself hypothetically in her care, sipping the comforting warm liquid in this otherwise unfamiliar new territory.

"I don't know," she hesitated. "What do you want to do?" she asked, emphasizing the word 'you.' And when I hesitated, taking a moment to reply, she continued, "I see three options here, depending upon what you want and what you are prepared to live with, or not prepared to live with, as the case may be. First, and the most dramatic, is to move out and file for divorce right away. The other extreme is to ignore the whole thing and carry on as if nothing has ever happened. But I don't think you would want to do that," she added, with a hesitation in her voice. "The third possibility is to confront him, talk it through and see if you can work something out, providing, of course, you both want to and are able to, after what has happened."

She's right, I thought. That leaves me two options: to say something or to shut up. Well, I knew that all along. I didn't need her to tell me that! Suddenly I felt resentful. How come she is so ordered and well organized, pontificating about what to best do? I thought and my suspicions grew stronger than ever. I started to feel like a hypocrite, sitting there with these thoughts knocking about in my head. I felt I had better leave.

"You're right," I said out loud to her. "It's simple, really. I just need to think it through and make a decision. Thanks for the tea." I stood up. My change of mood must have seemed abrupt to her.

"Where are you going?" she asked, responding to the sudden haste.

"I must get home. Just look at the time!" I said, glancing at my watch. It wasn't late at all and I knew Andrew wouldn't be home for some hours. If only I could listen in to her telephone conversations the moment I walked out the door. I felt sure she would be phoning him immediately to warn the perpetrator that they had been found out. We kissed on both cheeks, as we always did and said our goodbyes. I noticed her perfume—expensive, no doubt.

Back in the car, I dialed Andrew's office. "I'll put you through," said the receptionist and immediately I could hear the busy signal. The receptionist's voice came back on. "His line is busy. Do you want me to put you through to his voice mail?"

"No, it's all right, Anita. I'll talk to him later."

There it was—another proof, another piece of evidence. All right, I would take it all the way. I stopped at the nearest phone booth and looked up the hotel in the telephone book—the Golden Dusk. I phoned their office and asked for the address of the hotel. I was going to get to the bottom of this. Once I had the address, I worked out that it would take me about an hour to get there. I still had enough time to drive there and back before Andrew would come home. I dropped in to the house on my way and rummaged around in the box of photographs, where I found a picture of Andrew, Anne, Nick (Anne's current boyfriend at the time) and me, taken during last year's vacation in France. There we were in a vineyard in Provênce, tasting the grapes. How sun tanned and happy we all looked! How ironic! But it was a good, close up shot and you could clearly see Anne's features on it.

It didn't take me long to get out of town and the hotel was not difficult to find, as it was advertised on a billboard on the main road and was located at the edge of a small village, with a forest and a chain of green hills stretching out behind it. Set in its own grounds, it was very picturesque and clearly well cared for, with outdoor swimming pool, landscaped gardens with fountains, flowerbeds and a golf course. It had that quiet, stately atmosphere that makes you slow down and feel you have all the time in the world.

Once in the large foyer, which made you think you were in the tropical colonies, I walked up to the reception desk. An attentive clerk asked me if he could help me.

"I want to check something," I said, suddenly feeling self conscious and awkward. I pulled out the photograph. "I would like to know if this woman was booked in to your hotel on the night of September sixth."

The man looked at the photograph, then at me, incredulously.

"Madam," he said, "there are three hundred guests every night in this hotel. They come and they go all the time." As he spoke, a bellboy appeared behind the desk and as he reached for the key to one of the rooms, he craned his neck, trying to catch a glimpse of the picture. The clerk looked at him admonishingly and handed me the picture back.

"I can't possibly remember," he said and added, "sorry," in a tone that sounded final and clearly marked the end of the conversation. I felt crestfallen and stood there for a moment, not knowing how to proceed further. The clerk then leaned over the counter and added in a hushed voice, "Unless this is part of an official investigation, we pride ourselves on our discretion. We do not disclose guests' details to anyone."

"I understand," I replied as I put the photograph away. "Thank you for your time," I said, turning away and feeling that it wasn't all right at all and that I had just wasted my time. I slowly walked to the door.

As I left the hotel and made my way towards the car, I saw a figure approaching me from the side entrance to the hotel. It was the bellboy whom I had seen earlier behind the desk.

"I saw the picture," he said, as he approached me, "and I remember the girl," he added quickly, as if trying to hold my attention before I walked away. "She was here," he said firmly.

I opened my purse and pulled out a twenty-dollar bill.

"How can you remember?" I asked, handing him the banknote.

"I only remember because that was the day of my sister's wedding," he said, taking the money and putting it into his pocket with the speed of a true professional informer. "And I was due to be best man, so I was in a hurry to leave work. It was the end of my shift and I was really off duty, but those were the last guests that I was escorting to their rooms. You see, John, that's the guy who had the next shift after me, was late and I was filling in for him while he was getting changed into his uniform. I remember because we had an argument about it, but the manager asked me to stay on for half an hour longer, so I did. That lady—the one in the photograph," he added, "was being very fussy, asking me questions about the place, about meal times, pool times, gym times, even though it's all written down in the brochure. Then she got me to shift the suitcase from the stand to the bed, checked out the bathroom, the closet and the tea service. I remember her because I was almost late for my sister's wedding."

"You have an extraordinary memory," I said while thinking that it sounded just like Anne—fussy and very particular. She was, after all, a Virgo. I was convinced it had to have been her. Once again I pulled the photograph out of my purse and handed it to the bellboy.

"Are you quite sure?" I asked.

"Yes ma'am, I am certain," the boy said. "I hope that will be all. I've got to go now. I'm still on duty." He brought his two fingers up to his cap in a kind of salute, pivoted on his toe and began walking back to the entrance of the hotel.

I was left there, standing in the middle of the driveway, still holding that photograph from two years ago. So it is her, was all that kept reverberating through my head. It's her. Suddenly, in my mind Anne was the villain, the false friend, the husband stealer, cold and destructive, cruel and uncaring—the vamp, the femme fatale, the family breaker.

Chapter Two
Search for Help

My world shattered, I felt lost and sad, but strangely quiet and more at peace than I had felt since first discovering that fateful bill. Now I knew; now I was certain and with certainty came a certain determination. Now I had to act. It was for me to decide what to do. I had the evidence, I had the confirmation. After all, that had to be what I was looking for, as I had driven all this way to this hotel in the country. So now what? The three scenarios still presented themselves to me: walk away, make a scene or pretend nothing had happened. None of these seemed satisfactory and as I played them out in my mind, not one of them brought with it a sense of resolution. I felt I could not throw away three years of building a relationship, even if that relationship had turned out to be a joke. A scene seemed to be unpredictable in its results. He could either deny the whole thing, walk away or beg for forgiveness. Thus three further results presented themselves to me, depending on Andrew's reaction, though in each one I did not feel I would be in control. No, I must first make the decision myself; I must decide what I want to do, rather than wait first for his reaction and response.

The final solution, to go on as if nothing had happened, felt dishonest to myself and to Andrew and I didn't really believe we could continue like that for very long. Certainly not a good foundation for a relationship with the potential of stretching into the future. No, it simply would not do.

I still felt lost and confused, but accompanying these emotions there was also a quiet determination being born. I could see beyond this disaster into the future now and I realized that whatever I might decide, life would still go on and that I needed to think about what was next ahead and what I really wanted to do with the rest of my life. Up to this point I had depended on Andrew for most decisions; I had depended on him for most of my income, my well-being, my projections, even my ambitions and my desires. Whatever was to happen next, I realized I needed to discover who I was and what I wanted. That was the only thing that was becoming clear out of this whole mess. It was time to look ahead and realize that there was life beyond Andrew, after all, and that I would need to discover what that might be like. Whether our marriage survived or not, this issue still presented itself to me and I knew that I had to make up my mind who I wanted to be. That I could earn a living I did not doubt, as I trusted that there were many skills and abilities locked up inside of me, waiting for their liberation and appearance. After all, I could type, I could keep books, I could drive, clean, sew, decorate, cook... all the things I had been doing regularly and consistently for three years now or longer, I could do for others, or for a company, if they were prepared to pay me for it. I had many friends and acquaintances and although most of them were also Andrew's friends, I did not doubt that they would help me become established...

Interesting that I was thinking this way, as if I had already made up my mind. Perhaps my sub-conscious was trying to tell me something. I was driving through the town by now and motivated purely by instinct, I turned into a shopping plaza and parked the car. I was not ready to go home yet. Besides, Andrew wouldn't be back till late anyway—he was taking a couple of customers out to dinner. In the plaza there was a large bookstore and I had always enjoyed walking around it, picking up books randomly, trying to find something to read. I also enjoyed browsing through the art section and admiring the colorful reproductions of artists from around the world; it was also a good place to think about things in peace and to do a self-diagnosis, for I was always interested to see which books I became drawn to on any particular day. There was also a small café in the far corner of the store where they served delicious coffee and gourmet teas. This felt like a good time to indulge the sense of taste, which always seemed to bring with it a feeling of security, even if only for a brief moment.

I entered the store and, well familiar with its layout, I walked past the many display units, letting my eyes survey the new releases and slowly wandering towards the back of the store where the less colorful, more serious writings were located. I was already interested to see that I had not picked up a single volume with the intention of examining closer its contents. My mind was preoccupied, this was true, but I also felt I was in pursuit of a clue. I stopped in front of the section entitled Philosophy and Religion and stood there for a moment, looking through the titles on the shelf. Most of these books I had already seen before, and they included such titles as the classics of all the major religions, as well as what could be classified as New Age books, including writings on meditation, self help and spirituality. I didn't feel like picking up any of these volumes, until my eyes rested on a title that I had not seen before. Unlike the others, it was displayed with its cover facing the customer, its back resting against several other books on the shelf. It caught my eye because its cover was so colorful and it depicted a man in a white gown, gazing back at me with an intense look that seemed to reach deep within my soul (whatever and wherever that was). I had the strongest sensation that he was looking at me personally and that I had known him for millions of years, beyond this life and beyond recorded history. I smiled to myself as soon as I thought this thought, because it seemed so ridiculous to my educated mind, and yet the sensation that went with it could only be described as a *gut feeling*. There was also a command in his look, as if something was now required of me, as if there was something I absolutely had to do and my life and my future depended on it. I picked up the book and flicked through its pages. It was a collection of thoughts, exercises and meditations; the few I managed to read as I stood there in front of the bookshelf seemed very simple and easy to understand, yet inspiring and challenging at the same time. I flicked back to the beginning and read the dedication: "To those who are lost and know they are lost, for they are the precious few, as most of the world population are ignorant of their departure from the Truth. To those few blessed ones I dedicate this book in the knowledge that the great adventure of life awaits them as they search for their place in the world."

Yes, that's me! That's definitely me! I felt that the book had been personally dedicated to me. I looked back onto the shelf and saw that it was the only copy in the entire section. I even searched the neighboring sections, but couldn't find another copy. This one was mine, I knew it. Perhaps this was my imagination, but it was almost as if I felt a certain energy coming off the book and traveling up my arm, as I held it. The sensation was warm and pleasant; it was also tingly and began to radiate a certain well-being right through my body, and I felt I was already being healed.

I approached the cash desk and handed the book to the young salesman, almost concerned that he would not give it back to me. The computer would not register the book as he held it over the "magic eye" of the checkout. He tried several times, then shrugged his shoulders and typed in the information manually.

"I haven't seen this one before," he said and added, "It must be new."

And still, nothing came up on his screen, except an inscription, *item unknown*. He tried several times and then picked up a phone, at the same time explaining to me, "It has not been entered into the computer yet. I better call the manager." He spoke into the phone, asking for assistance.

I waited while he served another customer, my eyes on the book, as if I was afraid it would disappear. The manager came out of his office and approached the check-out counter. He picked up the book and turned it around in his hands, as if looking for a clue.

"I don't remember seeing this one," he said. "Where did you get it from?"

"From the 'Philosophy and Religion' section," I said, pointing to the back of the store. He looked in the direction of my pointing finger and said, almost as if he were issuing a challenge, "Show me."

We walked to the shelf where I had found the book and I showed him where it had been displayed before I picked it up. As ascertained before, there were no other copies available there.

"I don't understand," he muttered as we walked back to the cashdesk. He handed the book back to the young employee and said. "I can't find it. I don't know what it should cost. How about you charge ten dollars for it. Is that all right?"

I felt such relief—they were going to let me have it, after all.

"Yes, that's all right," I said, as I reached for my wallet and paid for the book. The salesman put it in a bag and handed me the package with the receipt and my change. It was finally mine!

I walked out of the store in such a different state from the one I was in when I had entered. Something in me had lightened and felt released, just as a bird that has been let out of a cage must feel. I went back to the car and sat behind the wheel, reading bits of the book, as I flicked through the pages.

Suddenly I noticed that there was an address at the back, with the following note: "If you want to know more about how to discover the truth about yourself and the world you live in, phone this number, or visit us at the following address..." I picked up my cell phone, but just as I tried to dial the number, the phone ran out of charge and the display darkened.

I frantically looked around for another phone. There was one right in front of me, at the edge of the plaza. I got out of the car with the book in hand and dialed the number, using my phone card, which I always carried with me in case of emergency.

A woman answered; she had a pleasant, rich voice and she seemed rather slow in her response, unlike most receptionists that I have dealt with in the course of my interactions with institutions, schools, companies and places of work. I told her that I had a copy of the book and that I wanted to meet the author, if that was at all possible.

"Yes, it is possible," she said. "He instructs and teaches during our annual retreats. There is one coming up soon. In fact..." she hesitated, as if she was looking up dates in a calendar, "...it starts tomorrow. If you come in today, you can have your interview this evening and start the course tomorrow. It's a one-week intensive residential retreat at our rural center just out of town. All you will need are some clothes and toiletries; everything else will be provided."

"I'll be there," I heard myself saying to my surprise and suddenly I felt I had a mission. I had put the phone down even before I had asked the price. Well, that didn't matter—I would pay whatever it cost; after all, I did have some of my own savings and this is what I would use them for.

I drove home and threw some clothes in a bag. I would be gone for a whole week! That felt good—it would give me time to think about my life, my marriage and what I intended to do. Andrew would be surprised, perhaps even upset, but he had been away so often himself, I felt it shouldn't really matter. If anything, it would give him the opportunity to think about our future as well. It would also demonstrate that nothing was the same between us any more. It would be a good move. I would not phone him, for he would want to dissuade me; I already knew that. This would be a test and we could either start again or drift apart at the end of it.

I sat down to write him a note—I explained where I was going but I did not mention the name of the place or the address or the telephone number. I simply told him that I needed to be alone and I needed time to think. That should be clue enough.

Well then, amazing how quickly things can change in one's life. I felt miles away from the woman I had been that morning, standing at the dry cleaner's, ready to get on with my daily chores. Here I was now, about to disappear into a retreat center and spend a whole week finding out more about who I was and who I was about to become. There was no one else I intended to inform about what was happening; this was something I was doing for myself alone, for my life and for my future. I needed to know the truth about me; I needed to understand what I was doing here on planet Earth and how I could do it better. I needed a clear distinction and a new beginning and I felt this was it.

And so my new adventure began, strangely phoenixed out of a very messy situation and I was soon on my way to I-didn't-know-what. It could be a con, it could be a fraud, and I could have been on my way to a disaster. But somehow I didn't think so. At any rate, I didn't feel I had a choice; I simply had to do this. And how strange that I actually could do it—I happened to have the time, the means and the will to do it.

I looked it up on the map—it seemed remote, accessible by a small country road only. I had never been in those parts before and I was already looking forward to discovering a neighborhood I had never seen before.

Chapter Three
Something Responds

I had been driving down a narrow country lane for some time and I was beginning to worry that I had missed it. The road was windy and hilly, with dense trees on either side and no sign of a house, a fence or a driveway. It felt claustrophobic because there was no break in the trees and I was not able to look long distance at all and, worse still, as I drove on and the elevation seemed somewhat higher, I could feel the pressure changing in my ears and the air was getting damper, with veils of mist rising from the forest floor and wafting across the road to suddenly appear as milky fog in front of the car. I had to slow down and I became aware that I had not seen another car for about twenty minutes now. If there was one coming the other way, there would barely be enough room for us to pass and we would both have to slow down almost to a halt.

As the mist thickened, I slowed down some more and was intensely peering outside the windscreen window in an attempt to make sure I was not veering off the road and trying hard to see whether I was passing any buildings or driveways, hidden from view in between the trees. But the landscape continued to feel deserted and lonely and the whole thing was becoming too impossible so I decided I had better turn back. I stopped the car and relaxed for a moment, having made the decision, wondering whether I could manage a three-point turn on this road, or whether it would need to be a five-point turn, or even a seven-point turn.

It was just at that moment that the sun pierced through the clouds, the mists cleared and the fog lifted, as if it had never been there in the first place, and before my astonished eyes a new sight emerged. I had stopped at the top of a hill and in front of me there was a short stretch of the road, leading downhill straight towards a large gate with a clearly visible sign upon it: HUMAN DEVELOPMENT RETREAT CENTER. Underneath the sign there was a doorbell and a smaller sign that I could not read from where I had parked. Feeling relief, I drove up towards the gate. The sign underneath the bell said, "Please ring"—I could see it clearly now, but before I had a chance to get out of the car and press the button, the gates swung open before me, clearly guided by electronic means, and I was soon driving up a tree-lined curved gravel path, with beautifully cared for lawns stretching either side. As I navigated a bend in the driveway, a large white building emerged before me, with several outbuildings on either side and behind it—gardens, lawns and greenhouses, stretching as far as the eye could see. In front of the building the driveway widened to accommodate several cars and I parked mine alongside a row of vehicles that were already there.

Well, if nothing else, then this was a beautiful spot and no doubt a stay here would give me ample opportunity to rest and repair and think about my future. I now was beginning to feel an excitement, as I faced the unknown and I was so glad that I had responded to the message in that book which I was now clutching, as I approached the door. I briefly marveled at the many coincidences that had brought me to this place, and the only word I could think of was *serendipity*.

However, I did not have time to ruminate long, for I was now standing in front of a very heavy oak door, with large brass hinges and a doorknob gleaming in the sunlight. Again, there was a doorbell and I rang it three times, wondering if anyone could possibly hear it. But yes—quite promptly the door opened and there stood before me a middle-aged woman in a grey dress with a string of pearls at her neck. She had a kind face and she looked as if she had been there for a very long time; somehow her beaming and the place seemed to go together well.

"Come in," she said, "we have been expecting you." And then, when she saw I was surprised, she added, "Mrs. Johnson, I presume?"

"Yes, that's me," I said, as I stepped into the large hallway and stood aside as she closed the door. The place felt large and clean, with a few paintings on the wall, which I could not understand—probably symbols of some kind.

"I am Mrs. Pearce and I am the administrator here," the woman said, extending her hand, which I shook vigorously. "We'll go into the office and I'll explain everything to you," she said, as she started making her way down a corridor leading off the entrance hallway. She stopped at a door to our right and opened it, then she held it open as we both entered and she closed it as soon as we were inside. We were indeed in an office—it was oak paneled and very quiet, with a couple of large oak desks, bookshelves covered with books and a couple of filing cabinets.

"Take a seat, Mrs. Johnson"—she pointed to a chair, as she sat behind one of the desks. "I'll just get the paperwork ready first." She opened a blue file that was lying in front of her. "So, you've signed up for our one week personal development course. It starts tomorrow, but the times and ways of it are as irregular and as unpredictable as each person is unique. The lessons will be designed specifically to your personal needs and neither you nor we will know from day to day how exactly it will unfold. You are free to go at any time, of course, but by doing so you will have broken the contract and the course will be discontinued. So while you are here, please stay within the grounds and do as you are instructed. Those are the rules—that is really it. Everything else depends on you and how you progress. And now, if you have any questions, please ask and then I will show you your room and the Retreat Center's facilities."

"You mentioned an interview over the phone," I said, "will that be taking place tonight?"

She glanced at the clock on the wall above the desk and replied, "Yes, in about an hour, as soon as you have had the time to unpack and settle in. It will be in the Pink Room, which I will show you in a moment."

She stood up and I took my cue from her. We proceeded to leave the office and travel back down the corridor, as she opened up various doors and explained:

"Here is the library, and here is a quiet room for meditation and thinking. There is no talking in this room. And here is a small meeting room, which is called the Pink Room. It is where your interview will take place tonight. And this is the dining room. All bedrooms are in the west wing. Your room is number two. It's the first on your right, as you enter. There is no need for a key; we don't use keys here. If you have any questions, please don't hesitate to ask. There is an internal phone in the room—just pick up the receiver and dial '0' and you will get through to the office."

She paused for a moment and added, "Dinner is at eight. Your interview is in an hour—that is at six. See you later."

We were by the door and the brief tour was over. She opened the door and smiled. I was just about to walk through the door when she spoke again and I stopped in my tracks. "One last thing," she said, "the course is a week, but it might appear to you to take longer. That is because time acquires different properties here. But don't worry. We will keep track of it for you and we will make sure that you return safe and sound when the week is over." I hesitated for a moment, wondering whether I should ask her more about this, but decided against it. It could wait. I didn't have to know everything within the first half hour. I smiled and walked through the open door back into the courtyard. I walked over to the car and retrieved my bag from the back seat. Then I proceeded to what was clearly the west wing—a long rectangular building, within which there was a central corridor with doors coming off both sides. My bedroom was the first on the right, as had been explained. I entered and inside I found a bed, a chest of drawers, a closet, a desk and a chair and in the corner a sink with a mirror. There was also an adjoining bathroom, perhaps added later, with a shower and toilet inside. I sat on the bed and as I sat there, I felt two sensations sweep over me—one was a feeling of relaxation and a draining away of all tensions, and the other was a strange excitement and enhanced feeling of being alive, that seemed to permeate my entire body.

By the time I had unpacked my bag, had a shower and sat down to gather my thoughts together, it was time to go. I did not want to be late for this interview; it seemed too important. I was dressed casually, because all I had brought with me were my jeans, a few different tops and some underwear. But it seemed important that I looked fresh and clean. I checked myself in the mirror and satisfied with what I saw, I walked out of the door.

The Pink Room had indeed pink curtains and the walls were painted a light shade of pink as well—it was a small room with a table and a couple of comfortable armchairs and two upholstered matching straight-back chairs. An intimate room, clearly designed specifically for interviews or small gatherings. I sat down in one of the chairs at one side of the table and proceeded to look around—there were a few pictures on the walls, representing scenes from different parts of the world: the pyramids at Giza, the Ka'aba at Mecca, Notre Dame in Paris, the step pyramid at Chichén-Itzá in Mexico, the Taj Mahal at Agra and the Great Wall of China—I was pleased with myself that I recognized them all, though I had not seen them all in person. I was beginning to wonder what this collection of monuments could possibly mean, when the door opened and a man walked in, dressed in a simple white, floor-length robe. I estimated he must have been in his forties, though it was difficult to tell for sure, as I looked into his firm yet serene face and very penetrating brown eyes, the kind that make you feel as if there are no secrets for you to hide from them.

He stood in front of the door and I stood in front of him. The moment seemed long and the silence uncomfortable. Finally, he broke it by saying, "Mrs. Johnson, I presume." He smiled, as if mocking his own words. We shook hands and I felt a power in his warm handshake that was not menacing, but reassuring.

"Please sit down," he said and I tried to place his accent, but I couldn't work it out at all.

We sat down on either sides of the table and I waited for him to speak, wondering what kind of questions I would need to answer to be admitted into the course. I did not have to wait long.

"Do you know why I am wearing a long robe?" he asked and I went completely blank. I did not expect this. He waited a moment and finally I came up with an answer, which did not feel satisfactory, even as I uttered it, "Because it has to do with your religion?" I made a feeble attempt, with no idea what religion would require the wearing of such an apparel.

"No," he replied, "it is because you expect it."

I had to think about this but his answer had affected me deeply and I felt my heart pounding, as I briefly wondered, how he could possibly know what I was expecting and why he would want to accommodate any expectations I might have. I did not realize that I had had any expectations, but then I remembered the nerves and the butterflies in my stomach and I had to admit, at least to myself, that yes, there were expectations.

"So you read my book?" he half stated and half asked.

"Well, no, I looked at it briefly and read parts. It seemed very applicable to my life now." It seemed important to be honest.

"That's why I sent it to you."

"But I bought it in a bookstore," I began to protest.

"Yes, I know," he said, as if the two statements were not contradictory in terms. He seemed thoughtful for a moment, and then he said, "The timing is good. I think you are in a place in yourself and at a time in your life when you will be able to appreciate the training that you will receive here. We shall start tomorrow. There will be twenty-one lessons during this first term. It will take as long as it takes, but as far as the world is concerned, you will be gone for only a short time. Then you will return to your everyday life and when and if you are ready, you may come back for a second term. That is, if you pass the test."

This sounded very strange to me. A test? What test? I must have looked surprised because he paused and added, "Our tests are nothing like the question and answer exams you take at school or university. The test you will be required to pass, if you are to be admitted to term two, is to do with living, attitude and the power of the mind." Another short pause and then he continued, "While here, you will be given instructions by me and if at any time you feel they are unreasonable or impossible to fulfill, you may simply leave and no questions will ever be asked about it. However, you will not be invited to attend term two if you do so." He paused for a moment.

"Have you got any questions for me?" he asked. I found it difficult to think.

"So when do we start?" I asked, surprised that I was not enquiring further about conditions, tests, his credentials, finances, or any such matters. I was eager to begin and wondered about the routine. I had already worked out that twenty-one lessons in seven days meant three lessons a day. He looked at me briefly and, as if responding to my thoughts, he said, "There is no fixed routine. Some days there might be five lessons; on other days there could be no lessons at all. It all depends on your response, application and absorption ability. The training will start tomorrow." He stood up and I followed his example. "I'll see you then."

The interview was over. That was it. He left the room and I was on my own again.

Part Two

Twenty-One Lessons

Lesson One
Your Unlimited Potential

The next day I was awoken by a telephone call to my room. "Good morning. This is Mrs. Pearce. It is seven-thirty and your first lesson will begin at eight, before breakfast. Please come to the office and I will show you where to go from there."

I was up, washed and dressed in a hurry. I felt expectant and excited. As soon as I arrived at the office, Mrs. Pearce directed me to the back door of the building, which led onto a terrace leading to steps descending towards a large, well-kept lawn. A few steps away from the building there were two chairs arranged opposite each other and there were a couple of objects on the ground between them. Mrs. Pearce motioned for me to occupy one of the chairs and as I walked towards it I could see that the objects on the ground were a tray with a decanter and a glass on it. As I approached the chair the Master seemed to appear, as if from nowhere and, having acknowledged my presence with a slight nod of the head, we both sat down. I looked at the tray on the ground between us and noticed that the decanter was full of water and the glass was empty.

"That glass represents your complete potential, as you sit there," he said. "Now take the water and pour into the glass the amount of potential you think you have already used up."

I looked at the glass, then at the decanter, then at him. I thought for a moment. I was 26 and perhaps, if lucky, I could expect to live to

80 or 90. Twenty-six into 90 or even 80 is less than three. I carefully picked up the decanter and filled the glass up by a third.

He picked it up, peered into it, visibly displaying disbelief and then he poured the entire contents of the glass onto the ground.

"No," he said, "you have hardly begun."

He handed me the glass and I looked inside, observing the few remaining drops, clinging to the walls and slowly traversing the glass surface to the bottom where a tiny pool of water was forming as I held the glass at an angle.

"That is the amount of potential you have used up. You have no idea how much you are capable of and you must not stop yourself by thinking that you know! Humans are born with the ability to be great in whatever discipline they choose to pursue, but mostly that ability remains dormant and unused. So the first lesson is for you to realize that even at 26 you can be much more than you have ever thought possible. Do not limit yourself by how you think about yourself—always try to push back the boundaries and limitations that others may put upon you, or, worse, that you put upon yourself, thereby lessening your God-given opportunity and heritage."

Lesson Two
Conformity

After lunch I was summoned to the terrace of the house where the Master was already waiting for me, seated in a chair and holding what appeared to be a blank piece of paper. I sat down in a chair opposite him and as I did so, he handed me the ordinary, lined sheet of paper.

"This is your next tasking," he said, "fold it."

I looked at the paper to see if there was some hidden meaning or writing, but I could detect nothing, so I obliged and folded the paper in half. I thought best not to let him wait.

"Done," I said, anticipating a lesson, as I held out my hand with the folded sheet. He did not take it from me.

"All right, fold it again," he said.

I folded the paper in half again. He spoke before I had a chance to say anything. "Fold it again."

I did so and the paper became an eighth of its original size.

"Now open it up," he said.

I did so and the paper in front of me had four creases going one way and one crease down the middle from top to bottom.

He took the sheet of paper from my hand, looked at it attentively and intensively for a few moments and finally he said, "Everyone folds a piece of paper like that—you are no exception and no different from any of my other students. And yet the human is born free and everyone is different, with different fingerprints and the ability to think for oneself and to be original, unique and special. I said, 'fold the paper,' but I did not tell you how to fold it. You could have folded it in a fan shape, in a triangular shape, you could have made a boat, a plane, an origami duck or anything else for that matter. You could have taken your initiative and torn the piece of paper as well, you could have scrunched it up to give it a three dimensional appearance, and yet, what did you do? You folded it three times along three intersecting lines. How limited and unimaginative, how boring, considering the vast capabilities of the human to think, to be adventurous, daring, to defy conformity. You could even have asked how I wanted you to fold the paper, if you thought a specific method of application was expected of you. You could have asked me why I had asked you to do it in the first place and what the object of the exercise was. But you didn't; in fact, you didn't think at all. This is what is the matter with the human race—they do not tend to think at all."

He took a short pause and then carried on, "If you want to develop your unique human faculties, you really need to learn to rise above the crowd and the terrible conformity that is holding the human in its vice-like grip and limiting its freedom of expression, thought and action. Especially in a circumstance where it is safe to exercise your individuality, where you are not breaking the law, disappointing anyone's expectations of you or going against anyone else's will. If you are to be anyone of merit at all, you are going to have to learn to be bold, to speak your mind, to dare to be different, to think outside of the box. There are over six billion people on this planet and no two are the same—even identical twins are not identical. If we all behave and think (or rather don't think) in exactly the same way, the human race will have no chance to progress into its next evolutionary stage."

With that he handed me back the offending piece of paper and looked at me with an ancient and very sad expression in his eyes.

"That's the end of today's lesson," he said, as he rose and slowly walked off, with a slight rocking movement to his step, as if his mind was already elsewhere.

Lesson Three
Deceitful Language

I was sitting in the dining room in the light of the setting sun when the Master approached my table and asked if he could join me.

"Of course," I replied. We sat in silence for what seemed a very long time, when suddenly I got the feeling that I needed to be elsewhere and that I should leave. I looked at my watch and was shocked at the time.

"It's late," I said, "I have to go."

He looked at me and with a smile that I was beginning to recognize as a herald of an oncoming lesson he replied, "People blame everyone and everything else, except themselves. It is in the very language that you speak. It, whatever it might be—time, the movement of the planets, the order of creation, is never late, but humans often are. When did you ever see the sun delayed because it had something else to do or a daffodil deciding that it would switch seasons and show up in the fall because it was getting fed up with spring and finding that the tulips got in the way and took away from its brilliant display? How can you say 'It's late,' when IT is so punctual that you can keep time by observing the stars or watching the rising sun?

"Your language deceives you. You claim that ever since Copernicus humanity and more recently even the church have accepted that the Earth revolves around the sun, yet you say 'the sun rises at 7:20' or 'that is a beautiful sunset.' The Earth revolves to face the sun every 24 hours and it would be more accurate to say so, or at least to know it and think it.

"Humans are so egocentric and geocentric and they see everything from a very personal point of view. When you try on clothes in a store, you say 'it is too small' or 'too big,' whereas it is made to be exactly the size it is. It is you who are too small or too big for it but who has ever heard a customer in a shoe shop exclaim as he or she tries on a new pair of shoes, 'My feet are definitely too big for that size. Can I try something smaller, please?'

"And what about the expression, 'warm clothes' or 'warm blanket'? They are not warm, but simply adjust to the temperature that surrounds them. A warm sweater, for example, is simply a piece of clothing that is thick enough to trap and contain the person's own body heat, thereby insulating them from their surroundings and not letting in the cold as quickly as a lighter item. Thus the warmth is self-manufactured, but the cloth contains it. So in this example we attribute our own warmth to inanimate objects that cannot possibly generate heat. It would be more accurate to say, 'That sweater traps my body heat for longer.'

"And what about a woman telling her friends that she is having a baby? It sounds so romantic, whereas in reality she is having a baby, an adolescent, a teenager and all the responsibilities that go with providing for a child and a child's education until it is old enough to look after itself. Somehow the phrase 'I am having a baby' does not reflect the depth of the change that is going to occur in that family when that child is born and for years to come.

"If you search, you will find many more examples of deceit in the language. Look for it and perhaps you will not be suject to deception elsewhere, above all in yourself and in your way of thinking."

And with that he stood up and left, before I even had a chance to reply.

Lesson Four
The Wall

One day I was walking through the garden, when suddenly I noticed that at the end of the pathway my way was barred by a wall. I could have sworn that just yesterday there was no wall there but now it was plainly visible against the autumn sky, each brick neatly laid. Just as I was contemplating how I could possibly get around the wall or jump over it, both of which seemed to me to be impossible tasks, the Master appeared in the distance, serene and smiling, unperturbed by the appearance of the masonry addition.

"The only way for you to get through that wall is to punch a hole in it with your fist," he said.

"How come?" I asked, disbelieving.

"It's a magical wall," he replied. It will only yield to strength, as most things in the world will. So you need to demonstrate your strength, no matter what the cost."

I thought about this for a while and realized it was a test. I looked at my fist and knew that it could not survive a serious encounter with a wall, any wall. And yet, I knew that if I were to progress, I must somehow come through this test. I closed my eyes and wished with all my might that it was all over, but when I opened them again, I was still standing confronting that damn wall.

"It's the only way," he said again with conviction, as if I hadn't heard him the first time.

This was the most difficult task yet. I was seriously thinking about giving up altogether when I realized that it could mean the end of training, the end of teaching, the end of my progress, which in turn would mean wastage of everything I had learned so far. At this moment what I had learned so far did not feel like much because I couldn't think of a single truth or lesson that I could draw upon to know what to do. Clearly he was testing my trust and dedication. I must therefore do it, I thought, if only to prove to him what a devoted student I am. I must believe that my education is more important than any bodily harm I might sustain. He does not want to hurt me— I know that; I am sure of it.

Finally, after several minutes of struggle, arguing with myself and hesitating, I finally made a decision. Yes, I would try. I would punch the wall. If my fist were to be broken at the end of the experiment, this was a small price to pay for the truth. I walked up to the wall decisively, faking courage, drew back my fist and smashed it into the wall... it turns out that the wall was made of rice paper and the bricks were in reality skillfully painted lines—my fist went straight through it, tearing a gaping hole in it and pushing through to the other side.

"You see," he said, "most walls are like that. They are rice paper obstacles which we see to be insurmountable obstructions with no more substance than a falling autumn leaf." He smiled and added, "I think you will now remember this tableau which was specifically created to convince you that most walls will disappear as soon as you make the decision that you will not let the difficulties confronting you stop you on your chosen path." He then further tore a bigger hole in the paper wall and motioned me to walk through it.

"Proceed with your stroll," he said as I walked through the gap and continued on my way.

Lesson Five
Appreciating Nature

I was walking through the garden, looking for the Master. I had been told that he was spending some time tending to his tropical plants. As I walked by the greenhouse at the end of the path, I could see a shadow behind the glass walls and I realized someone was in there, and I thought it must be him. I quickened my step and walked toward the glass construction in front of me. As I approached, I saw him through the open door. He was moving around amongst the many pots, bags of soil, compost and the watering cans. He was re-potting, replanting and looking after the many exotic plants that adorned the shelves, tables and stands in the greenhouse. It was a large, bright construction and it felt as if I had been transported into a tropical garden that was warm, moist and lush. He looked up from his task of adding soil to a large pot and smiled at me. I walked in and said, attempting to start a 'polite' conversation, "I've never seen a plant like that before. What is it called?"

"Brayera anthelminitica," he replied. "It comes from north-east Africa."

I knew I would never remember the name and immediately my attention was drawn to some slightly aromatic white flowers to my left.

"And what are these?" I asked, amazed at the great variety of vegetation, not seen elsewhere in local gardens or nurseries. He looked up and replied with a smile, "That is monsonia ovata," he replied.

"And where does it grow?" I asked.

"It is grown in South Africa," he said and turned his attention back to what he was doing. This went on for some time, in fact probably about an hour—I kept asking questions about the plants in the greenhouse, pointing now to one, then another. He patiently answered my questions, quoting complicated Latin names, places of origins, blossoming times, habits, habitats, needs and varieties. He knew a great deal about many plants and by the time the hour was up, I felt as if I had been reading a botanical encyclopedia with much information, many facts and names, but I was not much wiser than when I began.

My head in a spin, I turned towards him and, indicating that I wished to go now, I said, "Thank you for a very informative hour. That was really interesting and I learned a lot..."

I was about to say some other pleasantries, when he interrupted me, and said with a serious and concerned expression on his face, "You learned nothing. You asked me for information, names and places of origin. I obliged and told you about each plant that you wanted to hear about. At the end of the hour you've heard a lot of names and not much else. You probably cannot remember a thing and by tomorrow all this will be a distant memory. And yet you think you have learned something about exotic plants today. That's the problem with humans and their education system. They think that if they know the name of something, they know it. This is an illusion. If each of these plants were named differently, what difference would it make and would you then know more? No, you know nothing about these plants, just as knowing the date of a battle does not mean that a person knows anything about the story of what led up to it, the human emotions and sentiments involved or what it led to in the future.

"If you want to continue your work with me, you are going to have to learn to look behind labels into the real meaning of words and events. Knowing the name of something does not give you the knowledge of it or the power over it, even though you might think so. If you really wanted to know about these plants, you would spend time with them, watch them through the cycle of the four seasons, learn to cater to their needs and have a feeling life that would respond to their well-being. So, do not pretend you know. Begin today to look behind every name to the true understanding of what lives behind the label.

"Take this plant as an example." He held up a pot with a small plant covered with tiny delicate red flowers. "I think you will remember it far better if I don't tell you its name. It grows in the South African desert for a brief time, only once every two years during the rainy season. If there is a draught, it might not bloom at all for three, four or even ten years. But when it does rain, it will grow profusely within days and the entire landscape will be awash in crimson. If you were to name this plant, what would you call it?" I took a step forward and looked at the delicate flowers with growing interest. Each one had five petals with a cluster of yellow stamen in the middle.

"I think I would call it Red Beauty," I said and then added, "It is very beautiful."

"Good," he replied. "Perhaps you will learn to look at every plant, situation, emotion, person with new eyes. Try to ignore the labels and find your own definitions for things before you fix them with a familiar word or phrase. Learn to approach your life and everything you meet anew and you will become rich beyond measure."

After a moment of silence I realized the lesson was over, so I thanked him and quietly departed, leaving him to his plants, pots and gardening tasks.

Lesson Six
Variety

After breakfast the Master invited me into a room which I had never seen before. There, laid out on several tables, as if it was a Thanksgiving display at harvest time, was an array of many fruits and vegetables—anything I could have possibly imagined and many I didn't even know the name of. The variety was overwhelming; nowhere had I ever seen such a selection, even in the most expensive delicatessen where fruit and vegetables are imported from all over the world.

Every color of the rainbow was represented in many dramatic shades—from red peppers, strawberries, raspberries, tomatoes to oranges, carrots, bananas, lemons, grapefruit, limes, through asparagus, lettuce, many herbs, to grapes and eggplants, potatoes, yams, parsnips and so many more. All shapes, sizes and tastes—from sweet and delicate to strong and spicy. They were all there; in fact, I could not think of a single naturally growing food that was not represented.

I looked at him questioningly, not understanding what I was supposed to do with such an array of produce.

"I want you to answer one question," he said. "Contemplate why does the planet produce such an abundance. Take your time and when you have your answer, come to my office and tell me." With that he left me standing there, looking around, as if trying to find a clue. He obviously wanted me to think about this, so I sat down and started to repeat the question over and over and over again in my head. As I looked at the display on the tables, the multitude of shapes, sizes and textures, and above all the array of color—I thought of the theatricality of planetary display. My mind wandered to pictures of animals, birds and insects and everywhere I saw color and variety and display. I marveled at the many customs and habitats, the consequences of the change in climate over the centuries, which caused the appearance and disappearance of many species. This in turn led me to contemplate the ability of the human to learn from his or her environment.

As I continued to look at the fruit and vegetables, laid out in front of me on three large trestle tables, I began to notice and appreciate the many colors that nature bestows upon her produce. As I walked between the tables, I started picking out the colors of the rainbow— reds, oranges, yellows, greens, indigo and violet. There were no blue foods that I could see, but there were plums, eggplants, red grapes, red cabbages and other exotic fruit I did not recognize—all within the indigo and purple range. Then I started looking at shapes—leaf shapes, stem shapes, round fruit and vegetables, elongated spheres, egg shapes, even star-shaped fruit.

Such a variety and range. Third time around I looked at size and again I saw the smallest sesame seeds and the largest pumpkins—all produced by Mother Earth, all emerging annually from her soil in different parts of the world at different times.

At the end of the day the time came for my interview and as I knocked on his door, I was not at all sure of my response. I had a feeling and a new appreciation for what I had witnessed, but no reasoned answer to the Master's initial question. He asked me to enter and as I sat down, he looked inquiringly at me.

"Well," he asked, "what is the answer?"

"The planet is very theatrical," I replied, "and produces a multiplicity. It is her way."

He smiled and at that moment I knew I did not have the right answer.

"Yes, but why? That is the question," he said and added, "Can you answer that?" I fell quiet and shook my head from side to side. I didn't know. "Go back tomorrow and try again," he said and I obediently stood up to leave, wondering what revelations the next day would bring.

The next day there was a fresh display and the variety of produce was even more stunning and inviting; I almost felt like eating it all. But I resisted and sat down on a chair in front of one of the tables, ready to contemplate what my eyes were feasting upon. There were so many kinds of fruit and vegetables that I did not even know where they all came from. Some I did recognize and I knew some of the exotic names, which I had learned at various times in my life, when a new fruit was imported and displayed at the local store. Thus I knew that the kiwi fruit came from New Zealand, bananas from Israel or Mexico, and passion fruit from Africa. I knew how to eat a pomegranate or a pear or a lychee from China. It occurred to me that different parts of the planet are conducive to growing different varieties of vegetation, according to the climate, the amount of sunlight and rainfall, the wind, the temperature and the vacillation of these conditions. And just as each land has a frequency that promotes different accents, dialects and customs in its inhabitants, so the many parts of the planet give rise to endemic trees, flowers, fruit and vegetation. Humans have made these growth patterns less distinct by transporting seeds and produce and by growing vegetation that originated on one part of the globe onto another. I wondered how that would influence local conditions, perhaps eventually changing the climate, the behavior of humans and even the destinies of entire nations.

By the end of the day, having been on a whole journey in pursuit of the answer to the question concerning the variety of nature's vegetation and produce, I was confident that this time I had it. I boldly knocked on the Master's door, went in and sat down in front of him. I was prepared to give him a lecture.

"Every piece of fruit or vegetation, just like all organic life on Earth, processes a frequency on behalf of the planet. That is what organic life is for. And just as every district, every land and every locale has its unique radiation, so does a fruit or a vegetable. That would also explain the color and texture and shape—each is tuned in to a force or a power and processes it on behalf of the planet. The

Earth needs a varied diet of many radiations to continue in good health and thus the vegetation takes in force from the atmosphere, some of which arrives here from outer space, and translates it into physical matter and shape and form and definition."

I was thrilled that at last I had the right answer. Again, he smiled at me and said, "That is very interesting and you now have part of the answer. But you need to go back and contemplate the question again so that you may gain a deeper understanding of the relationship between humans and nature's produce." I felt crestfallen and I am sure my disappointment showed. I had been sure I had the right answer! I was so proud of myself that I was able to contemplate the unseen properties of all vegetation and that I now understood about different parts of the world hosting different universal frequencies. What more can there be to discover about this? But I said nothing, trusting that tomorrow would bring the next level of answer.

So, the third day came and again I went to the room of contemplation and again I encountered a fresh array of planetary produce. This day I had given up; my brain was tired. I no longer knew what to think; I had run dry of ideas. I looked and I looked and all I could feel was awe and inspiration at such variety. I realized I would probably be stuck in this room forever, trying to figure out the answer, but then it became clear that as long as I was alive on this planet, I was, as in this room, facing the table of plenty that the planet provides each and every day, each and every season. I felt moved and privileged. This was sufficient for me to live an enriched life.

In the evening I was reluctant to leave my contemplation, but it was time and I knocked on the Master's door for the third time. I felt humbled and full of well-being.

"I have no answer," I said, "but I have something far more powerful than that: I have an awe and a fascination for the great variety that the planet lays out before me. I feel rich beyond measure and privileged to live in such a varied, beautiful and theatrical place."

"Then," he said, "you have learned this lesson well and need to go to the room of 'The Contemplation of the Bounty' no more, for you will carry it with you wherever you go. Remember this feeling and you will always be grateful that the Great Mother provides for you and supports you each and every day."

Lesson Seven
Thirteen Beads

The Master woke me up early the next morning. He asked me to dress quickly while he waited outside my room and when I was ready, he told me to follow him, which I obediently did. He led me down a corridor, which I had never even noticed before, into a small room. As he opened the door the light that was streaming through a large window looking onto the garden hit my unadjusted eyes. I squinted and as they slowly came back into focus I noticed a table and a chair in the middle of the room. As we approached I could see that on the table there were thirteen colorful beads that looked as if they were made out of precious gems and gold and silver; in fact, there was one for each color of the rainbow, one black, one white, one pink, one deep purple and as mentioned before, one silver and one gold—thirteen in all. There were two other objects on the table—a needle and thick thread that looked like upholstery thread, with a knot tied at the end of it.

As I surveyed the scene, he started to speak, "Your task is simple. Thread these thirteen beads onto the thread in whatever order you like. That is it. You have three hours to perform this task and I will come back after your time is up to see how you are getting on. He started moving towards the door. My mind was racing. Three hours to thread thirteen beads? Why on earth do I need so much time? It did not make sense. I needed to ask quickly because in a few moments he would disappear behind the door.

"Is there any other instruction?" I asked. "What is the significance of the order of the beads?"

He stopped and turned around with a smile, as if he were indulging a stubborn child.

"The order is up to you. It is for you to work out." And with that he turned away, calling out as he departed, "I'll be back in three hours."

Well, that was that then. I sat down at the table and looked at the beads, trying to see some significance in the colors. They looked very pretty with the sun shining through them, throwing colorful shadows on the white tabletop. I picked each one up in turn, trying to contemplate its color and significance. I was beginning to understand that nothing here was done without reason, so no doubt each color had a meaning and a relevance as well.

I then laid out the seven that represented the rainbow colors— red, orange, yellow, green, blue, indigo and violet. This I knew how to do; I remembered the name ROY G. BIV from my childhood lessons. The rainbow is formed by the breaking up of white light—I therefore proceeded to place the white bead in front of the seven. Black is the opposite to white, so I placed the black bead after the seven. I still had four left over. So then I tried to add similar colors in what I thought was their appropriate places—pink between the white and the red, purple between the violet and the black. Then I still had the silver and gold left over. I spent the first hour and a half playing with the beads, trying this system or that idea, bringing colors together, then placing them apart. What was the right way to do this? I had no idea. Whatever I did, I then doubted what I had done and always some bead seemed to clash with another. For example, the metallic colors did not seem to belong with the rest and the black always seemed to stand out. Whoever brought these colors together, must have made a terrible mistake. Towards the end of the second hour the exercise was becoming very frustrating indeed!

I then took a break and thought of color and what I knew about it, how it appeared in nature and how on this planet there seems to be such a predominance of blue (the sky and the water), green (vegetation) and white (snow and clouds). The yellows and reds and oranges appear in nature in small amounts—vegetables, fruit, birds, flowers, except in the fall when of course the leaves turn to these colors as they dry up. At this point I realized that if green is made by the mixture of blue and yellow, then as the blue water retreats from the leaves, it is not surprising that the leaves turn yellow! I then looked at the sequence of the rainbow colors again and saw that green, which is in the middle, is made by the mixing of the blue and the yellow which are on either side. Orange, too, is made by the mixture of red and yellow, which are on either side. I then deduced that indigo must therefore be a mix of blue and violet on either side and violet must be a mix of indigo and red from either side. Now I understood why in art books the rainbow colors were always graphically represented as a wheel. I also could clearly see why the only three prime colors in the rainbow are red, blue and yellow—the three indivisible colors that are not formed by mixing two other colors.

At this point I was getting quite excited by these discoveries and would have been happy to carry on in my revelations, but I realized that time was ticking on and I still had not performed the task that I was asked to do. Funny, how I thought this was the simplest task yet and that it should take only three minutes maximum to perform, and here I was, two and a half hours later, still not ready. I wondered what to do and I just could not think of a *right* way to perform this task, so I decided that I would need a different criterion to go about it. Should I thread the colors in order of preference? I asked myself, or should I try a random approach and close my eyes to do this? The longer I thought about it, the more difficult the decision seemed to become. As the time kept passing by, I felt a gradual sense of surrender and then, virtually at the last minute, I went back to the very first idea with the rainbow sequence, adding in the other colors as I saw fit and adding the silver and gold at the end of the thread. Thus the task was performed, but I was not at all settled with the way of it and for the last few minutes of the third hour I awaited with uneasy anticipation for the Master's return.

He was punctual and within minutes he opened the door and walked straight up to the table.

"Ah, good," he said. "You have done it. I suppose you wonder what is the correct order and what is the lesson to be learned from this task?"

"Yes," I replied. "I am very curious. I couldn't work it out at all."

"That is good," he said. "You are not supposed to, because there is no *right* way. You were simply supposed to perform the task. There was no hidden significance to the order in which you may have chosen to place the beads, except that that sequence reflects your thinking process and character. However, there is a significance to the number of beads," he added. "If there were fourteen beads, there would be eighty-seven billion, one hundred and seventy-eight million, two hundred and ninety-one thousand two hundred possible variations of sequences in which you could have thread the beads. With thirteen, however, there are as many as six billion, two hundred and twenty-seven million, twenty thousand eight hundred variations possible. Thus approximately one possible variation for each person alive on Earth at this time. And you expect there to be a 'right' way? If I had each person alive come into this room, they could still do it in such a way as never to repeat the sequence."

I looked incredulously at the thirteen beads. Just thirteen beads and more than six billion people could attempt at putting them in sequence and it would have been possible for each one of them to never repeat the pattern? And I was looking for logic in my arrangement? No wonder no two trees look the same, no to leaves, no two cats, no two people. In fact, I realized, no two humans who have ever lived have looked exactly the same. With the exception of identical twins, but even then, their mothers can always tell them apart. In fact, I knew two identical twins and even I could tell them apart. Once you got to know them, you realized that they were, after all, very different indeed. So how many 'beads' were there in the DNA chain and what the chances of ever repeating the sequence? These questions seemed quite boggling and I felt the need to be alone to contemplate in solitude the vastness, the intelligence and the variety as displayed in the universe and in the world around us.

He seemed yet again to read my thoughts. "You may go now and think about this," he said with a smile.

Lesson Eight
The Bus Stop

T he following day we left the grounds and walked through the gates which I remembered from the day of my arrival. As we walked down the dusty road, I felt something change. The air became misty and saturated with moisture and as we proceeded, I could see less and less clearly—all this within the distance of a few hundred yards.

He began to speak: "We are going to walk to the bottom of the road, no further. By the time we get there we will have entered another dimension, where time does not exist. Never attempt to do this on your own—it is dangerous. But when you develop, you will be able to see beyond time on an ongoing basis and then, everything you look at will present itself together with its history. Thus, a book will reveal the ways and behaviors of the author, as he or she prepared it for print; the apple will testify to the whereabouts of its mother tree and the characteristics of the person who picked it; the candle will still be connected to the room in which it was made; the cup or vase will tell a story of the potter and the wheel where it was born...

"You will not be able to look at another person without knowing their history, thoughts, intentions and desires. In a way wisdom is a curse, for you cannot walk away from it and plead ignorance once you have it. You will always know if someone is lying to you, if they are a false friend and if they wish to harm you or simply take advantage of you. Imagine what it would be like to look at a person and know their weaknesses, their diseases and flaws—mental, emotional and physical. What would it be like to then struggle with the morality of not being able to tell them what you see or not being able to offer help unless you are asked? These are the dilemmas I face every single day."

This was the first time I had heard him talking about himself and I understood that he was letting me know what it could be like for me, too, if I continued along this path. It caused me to become silent as I contemplated my future and awaited this new revelation with growing expectancy.

"Today I shall give you an experience you will never forget. After that it will be your choice as to whether you wish to proceed further or not. And if you do, realize that your life will never be the same again and people will both admire and revile you and you will become lonely. But that is the price you will have to pay."

At that moment we started to turn a corner and there, further down the road I could see the bus shelter and within it what seemed to be crowds of people. I could see men, women and children, even dogs and many baby carriages. What was extraordinary was that there were so many in such a small space, they seemed to be virtually one inside the other, as if made of mist or gas, semi-transparent, ghostly, but nevertheless very real.

"See that bus shelter," he said, as he slowed down his pace. "It hasn't been there long—perhaps a couple of years. In that time five buses a day have stopped here and it is not at all a busy place. Yet what you are looking at now is a trace of all the people who have ever used that bus stop—men, women and children. They are all there, for they have left their mark in this place."

Slowly we came to a halt and we stood there for a moment observing the bus stop from a slight rise in the road. Suddenly I saw a figure standing outside the shelter at the side of the road, in amongst a crowd of virtually hundreds. The figure looked familiar and in a moment I realized I was looking at myself, waiting for the bus on the day before when I went into town for lunch. Not only could I see myself, but I could also clearly see my thought process and I knew I had been worried whether I would be able to complete this journey I was currently on. It made me fleetingly wonder what other marks I had left in other places. I realized that if I could read my thoughts from a day ago, so could he.

As if reading my thoughts, he said, "Yes, you are there too. And forever that moment, just like every other moment, is captured and preserved, like an insect in amber. It is stored here and accessible to anyone with the eyes to see and the mind to understand." As he was speaking, the scene slowly disappeared, dissolving into the mist. I realized the spell was broken but I would now always know that this was truly possible and that everywhere I went there would always be a trace of history left behind by those who had been there before, and that I would be leaving my own mark in each place I visited, to become part of its history and permanent unseen record.

Lesson Nine
Sharing

This day was different. The Master came to fetch me early and as we walked down the corridor towards the main hall, he explained that today, for the first time since I had entered his retreat, I would be working together with another student of his who was on a similar course as myself. The man was already in the hall as we entered and as the Master appeared in the doorway, the young man stood up from his chair, obviously awaiting his instructions.

"There is a task for you to perform," he said, as he reached for his note pad, which he was carrying under his arm. He proceeded to tear out a piece of paper as we both watched eagerly, wondering what would come next. He then bent over and carefully placed the piece of paper in the middle of the floor. "Imagine that you both want to stand on this piece of paper..." He looked at us and saw the doubt which appeared on both our faces. He smiled and explained further, "I know it takes a stretch of the imagination, but try. Let's just pretend that for some reason the prospect of standing with both feet on this piece of paper is very attractive to you both. You both want to do so more than anything in the world." We both nodded and he was clearly satisfied that he we now understood the rules of the game and that we were entering his world of make-belief and beginning to adopt its reality as our own.

He continued, "Now, clearly there is room for only one pair of feet on this piece of paper. Whose is it going to be? How are you going to resolve this conflict? What are you going to do?" We both looked at him, still trying to understand.

"I think I have made myself clear," he added. "I will therefore leave you here on your own for two hours. That's all you've got to solve the problem which, I hasten to add, is an ancient one. How are you two, students of the truth, going to resolve a territory struggle like this?"

As he left the room we looked at each other and clearly a thousand thoughts passed through each of our heads. I don't know what the young man that stood opposite me staring at the floor was thinking about, but I knew right away that I could not win in a struggle, for he was clearly stronger than me. Anyway, I did not feel that we should fight over who should stand on a piece of paper. The thought actually amused me and I smiled to myself. The man lifted his eyes at that moment and caught my smile, which embarrassed me.

"The name is Peter," he said. "And I'm not going to fight you over this," he said with a certainty that impressed me. I felt that he was further advanced than me and that he was someone who was not easily ruled by his emotions or by the need to win at all cost. I wondered if he, too, was comparing himself to me, both as far as strength and his own advancement were concerned. Well, if he was so knowledgeable, perhaps he had the solution?

"No, I don't intend to fight either. In fact I am perfectly willing to let you stand on the piece of paper." The whole thing seemed ludicrous to me. If he would agree, we could complete the tasking within a few minutes.

"Well thank you," he said and I was sure I could detect a hint of sarcasm in his voice. "That is very kind of you, I'm sure. But somehow, I don't think that is a realistic solution. We are not here to be courteous to each other or to learn manners. We are here to learn to be effective and real."

He clearly was ahead of me. Thus, perhaps I should submit to his ideas, for it seemed as though was heading towards some sort of solution. Or should I try to think for myself, which was something I wasn't doing very well at the moment?

"What do you suggest?" I asked, hoping that he might have the answer, after all.

"Well," he replied with a slight hesitation, "we could negotiate. Isn't that what countries do when they search for a peaceful solution to a territorial struggle? Didn't Napoleon sell Louisiana to Jefferson following lengthy negotiations?"

That last example really made me laugh, but outwardly I only smiled. After all, I never thought Louisiana was Napoleon's to sell, but I decided to let his comment pass without disputing it.

"Do you mean to say that I should buy the right to stand on that piece of paper?" I asked.

"Not necessarily," he replied, "but there must be a way that we can come to some agreement. Perhaps there is something you could offer me that would entice me to give up my rights to this paper territory. Or perhaps there is something I can offer you."

What could he possibly have that I would want? At this moment, all I wanted was for the whole thing to be over with. I didn't feel it was going very well.

"Like what?" I asked, only mildly interested.

"I don't know. I guess I would have to find something you might be interested in. Perhaps you can be tempted by some knowledge that I might be able to share with you."

"I don't think so. And it's not because I am not interested in what you might have to offer by way of knowledge. But somehow that doesn't feel right. Why should I give up my rights to this piece of paper in exchange for some information that I could probably find in a book or on-line anyway?"

"Perhaps because you know you can't win anyway. And therefore you might as well take the best advantage you can from a bad situation. And by the way, don't assume you can so easily find in a book or on-line what I have to offer by way of hard-won experience."

This was definitely not going very well.

"Perhaps I should just let you stand on it, as I recognize your superior strength. There is nothing I want from you. So I might as well surrender magnanimously."

"That is certainly a solution, but I am not sure it is the best possible solution."

"I don't see why we should look for the best possible solution.

Anything that gets us out of here is good enough for me." Listening to myself speak, I was beginning to see myself as stubborn, obstinate and downright rude. This sudden realization caused me to hesitate and moderate my stance.

Peter must have made a similar observation, for he responded with a question. "But aren't we here to learn?" he said. "In my experience nothing so far has been obvious and I don't think this lesson is any different. There must be a lesson here somewhere. If we find it, we will no doubt both benefit from it."

"I think the lesson lies in our finding a peaceful solution to the problem. Amicable would be the word, I think." I responded.

"So, what do you suggest?"

"I suggest we take turns. That way we both get a chance to fulfill our desires and we find a mutually agreeable solution. What do you say?"

He hesitated and I could see that he wasn't sure. Perhaps he felt the solution was a compromise, but in the end I persuaded him that it was the only way. We then needed to negotiate how long our turns would last and who would go first. Thus, the two hours went by quickly and we were still ironing out the final details of our mutually acceptable agreement when the Master returned.

He looked at what we were doing, sitting at the table, writing out our conditions and agreements and he must have understood in an instant what was going on.

"I am glad you are not fighting over this. But you have missed the point," he said and we both looked up from where we were sitting, the piece of paper abandoned in the middle of the room.

"The only way to decide who should have priority is to first find out what are your reasons for wanting to stand on the piece of paper. Once you know the reasons, you can easily decide which are superior. For always the good of the whole is greater than any personal interest. Thus the survival or well-being of the community is of greater importance than that of the individual or the family; the prosperity of the country is more important than any individual or group interest. Always look to the reasons, not the results and always struggle to have a greater view, encompassing as many considerations as possible."

Lesson Ten
Blades of Grass

It was a beautiful day—it had rained during the night and now the sun was shining and there was a very soft warm breeze blowing through the branches of the tall pine trees, bringing with it the fresh scent of an early fall day. I walked out into the garden and felt glad to be alive, glad to be witnessing the coming together of the warmth, the breeze, the smell of recently cut grass and the trees. All colors seemed more vivid than ever, with the bright blue sky gently merging over the horizon with the green and yellow fields in the distance. I was walking down a pathway, thinking of nothing in particular, except enjoying the day, when I saw the Master in the distance, walking towards me. His steps looked purposeful and it seemed to me that he had spotted me and was walking deliberately in my direction. Sure enough, he soon drew closer and I knew for certain that he had something in mind for me. I stopped in my tracks and awaited his approach.

"Come with me," he said and I followed him, as he led me towards the meadow that opened up beyond a line of trees to the right of the path I was walking along. Soon we stood ankle deep in fresh grass, still damp from the night's rain, with the water evaporating quickly. "I have a task for you," he added and then continued as I awaited his instructions. "I want you to sit in the grass and examine each blade that surrounds you very closely. When you think you have found each one's distinguishing characteristics, something that makes it different from all the other blades of grass, name it, give it a name that suits it according to what you see. I will return by noon to see how you are doing."

With those words he left, leaving me to my own devices. This seemed like an easy task and I sat down on the ground which was almost dry by now, warmed by the rays of the morning sun, and set out fulfilling my given task with enthusiasm and alacrity. At first all the blades of grass looked alike, for how could they be different—all more or less the same height, tapered off at the end, the same shade of green...? But no, soon I realized how wrong I had been and the longer I looked, the more I saw the differences. So soon the names started to roll off my lips: there was Bendy and Shorty and Thickster and Spotty and Patchy and Bright One, Crumpled and Yellow and Lonely and Torn and Straight, Sandy, Muddy, Shiny, Darky, Wetty, Feeble, Midget, Murky, Shady, Sunny, Glassy, and even the twins, Split and Spike. I was running out of names because I had limited myself to adjectival descriptions, when I realized that blades of grass had more character than just shape, size and color. This was a revelation and I imagined what it would be like to be the size of an ant, and to walk in amongst the blades of grass, as if they were trees, forming a shady forest. Thus a whole new supply of names opened up before me: there was Poplar and Plentiful, Pine and Bushy, Tinged and Ivy, Martial and Maple and Sword and Fever. At this point I realized that I could let my imagination take over and ascribe names to each blade that I instinctively felt would fit, a bit like naming a dog or some other pet. Thus amongst the blades there now appeared Mister Weighty, Summer Mist, Proud Junior, Tiger Lily, Fenced In, Dark Baby and even Emerald Jewel. At this point I started thinking of shades of green and a new batch of names appeared: Key Lime Prince, Peridot Midget, Hunter's Aim, Grassy Knoll, Spinach Column, Leafy Point, Pepper Peter, Pea Soup and Pale Kale. I was really enjoying myself, almost making friends with the individual blades, getting lost in the exercise, finding all kinds of little details to look for, like height, width, the surroundings, the neighboring blades, shades of green, imperfections, spots, splits, bends, discolorations, damp patches, traces of bugs or other creatures. I was so preoccupied with the task that I never noticed that the sun had climbed high in the sky and that the Master would soon be back. When he did arrive and approached the patch of grass where I was still sitting, he handed me a bottle of water. I hadn't even realized how thirsty I had become. I drank quickly and eagerly. He did not need to ask me how I got on, for I was so full with the experience of the past few hours, that I could not wait to share my discoveries, and thus outpoured my thoughts and ideas, as well as the examples of names given...

He listened very patiently to everything I had to say and when I finally finished, he smiled and made the following comment, as we walked slowly back towards the house, "The planet produces an abundance and nothing is ever exactly the same. No two days are alike, no two people, no two oranges, no two leaves, no two blades of grass. A wise person knows this and appreciates the difference. A wise person would never assume that another human being thinks the same as they do or will act as they would think it is prudent to act. We are all different and, like those blades of grass, we each display different characteristics, different preponderances, different ways, styles, different fingerprints and different genetics. It is an art to appreciate the variety and the differences, rather than insisting that all humans should think in the same way or that we are the same. We are not. Be proud of the difference and never suppress your feelings and thoughts in order to comply with the crowd. Who are you to judge who is right or better or wiser? You are unique and you can only fulfill that uniqueness by being yourself. It is for you to discover what that means and nobody else can do it for you. Time is limited for this great tasking that is placed upon you by the fact of living a life; it is for you to discover what that means for you. Think about it."

With this the Master left me to my further contemplation.

Lesson Eleven
Misfortune Cookies

I was sitting in the little meditation room, contemplating my life so far, above all the events that had brought me to this place of tranquility and peace. I realized with surprise that I had not had one thought about my domestic situation or my future needs since I had arrived here and I understood that this was like a pause taken within my life to re-examine my attitudes, stances and priorities. How lucky I was to have found this place and to begin to learn about myself and my life.

As I continued thus in contemplation, accompanied by the gentle trickling of the small fountain, the Master entered and sat beside me. He was holding a wooden box, elaborately carved. He sat in silence, as if giving me time to come out of my meditative state, and then said, "It would seem that you want to know more about yourself. So be it then. What I have here is a collection of what I call misfortune cookies. They are small pieces of paper with descriptions of various unfortunate qualities that a person might have. It is for you to pull three of them out of the box and to tell me whether the statement is true or false. That's all. There is no need to get upset or angry or heated—just consider the statement and let me know whether you agree with it or not."

Already I could feel panic setting in and I wasn't at all sure why. Somehow I felt on trial, though I knew this exercise was for my development and because I had requested this process in the first place. It seemed very important not to show my nerves or lack of confidence, but I detected a slight tremor as I held out my hand to choose one of the tightly rolled pieces of paper. I tried to be decisive and not to hesitate, picking one of the pieces of paper from the top of the box. Slowly I unrolled the note and read out the contents, "Sometimes you are rude," I read out slowly, trying to think about the statement as I read it.

"True," I added and I found that this was not too difficult to admit to. I reached for the next one, feeling somewhat relieved. I noticed that I was unrolling it slightly faster, with more confidence.

"You are lazy," I read out and this time it really felt as if the statement was directed at me. I wondered if all the pieces of paper in the box were about me. This one was not so easy to admit to, though I knew it was true. Before I could stop myself, I had said, "Sometimes."

"No," he interrupted. "Just agree or disagree. Either it is true or false. Nobody is anything all the time," he added, with the emphasis on the word 'all.'

"True," I said, noting that my voice was a little bit shaky as it came out and that I felt as if I had a lump in my throat. One more to go—I reached out again and I felt that the best thing to do would be to simply agree with whatever I pulled out of the box. If nobody is anything all the time, then perhaps everybody is everything some of the time, crossed my mind, but I could quickly think of a few things I definitely was not, like tyrannical or deliberately deceptive. All this happened in a few seconds, just as long as it took me to pick out another piece of paper and begin to unroll it.

"You are hard on yourself," it said. I quickly added, "True." No hesitation needed this time. I felt relieved it was over, but noted that my peaceful contemplative state from before the exercise had changed into a state of feeling sorry for myself, slightly emotional and with the beginnings of a doubt whether I would ever be of any account to myself, to him, to the world or to anybody else.

He must have sensed my change of mood, for he was quick to explain, "You must get to know yourself better. It does not mean that you have to eliminate such qualities as laziness, rudeness or the tendency to be hard on yourself. But know that that is what you are like. Learn to settle to who and what you are, for then you will be able to do something about it. There is nothing wrong with being hard; in fact sometimes it can be very useful to be hard, if, for example, you need to deal with a difficult person or assert your position when dealing with opposition. But if that hardness rules you, then you become subject to it and you will most probably be hard when you do not intend to be or would rather be soft. Thus observe yourself often, as if you were watching somebody else and learn about yourself; try to name your qualities, especially when you get emotional or upset. That is when you show your true colors most clearly, for on most occasions we tend to play a part and then we falsely convince ourselves and try to convince others that our role playing is the truth."

He paused and closed the box. "I will ask you to choose from my box of misfortune cookies again," he added as he got up to go. "Three is enough for today. As you become stronger, I will ask you to pull out a greater number from the box. The next batch of qualities will be a little more difficult to identify and harder to admit to."

With those words he stood up and walked out of the room. As he did so, I was convinced that all the pieces of paper in the box were specially designed for me, and it caused me to wonder what the other qualities written on the other pieces of paper could possibly be.

Lesson Twelve
Birth and Death

I was sitting on the terrace, sipping a cup of coffee when it came upon me to ponder about life and death. Here I was, what seemed to be five or six days into the process and the time seemed to be going so fast. I felt that already I had changed and that I was no longer the same person that drove through the gate on that very first misty morning.

Day by day I was moving closer to my departure and, by the same token, further away from my arrival, called birth, my childhood and the carefree days of my teenage years.

I did not hear the Master come up to my table and quietly sit down, as if he did not want to interrupt my reverie. When I did notice him, with a start, he smiled and said, "Ah yes, it is useful to ponder one's life journey. But beware of regrets. They will get you nowhere. Here is a way of thinking about your life that will help you steer away from regrets and guilt, the two enemies of progressive meditation and contemplation.

"The two major signposts of life, the two gates that everyone, absolutely everyone has to go through, are called birth and death—B signifying the beginning and D signifying the demise. Somehow in this modern culture of yours birth has come to be known as a joyful occurrence, with celebrations, congratulations, gifts and excitement, whereas death is seen to be a mournful, grief-stricken event, full of tears, crying and despair. If only you could reverse your thinking and see that life is a journey and that you came from somewhere and are going somewhere. Then you will see that as you are born, so you must have died elsewhere and as you die, so you will be born elsewhere. Thus if you could only substitute in your mind the word 'death' for the word 'birth' and the word 'birth' or 'rebirth' for the word 'death,' then perhaps your attitude would change towards these two inevitable milestones of a life's journey. The first is already done and completed and you cannot change the time, place or method of its occurrence. Anyway, you were not fully conscious when it happened and thus you were subject to the cycles and natural rhythms that govern physical birth. However, your death is another matter and you have yet to look forward to it, for it awaits you at the end of your journey. You can decide how it is going to be and prepare to meet it. The choice is yours. A conscious, well prepared departure is an excellent overture for what is to come. Imagine that as you were born and your birth was celebrated by family and friends, elsewhere in the universe your departure was mourned, as it was known that you were going on a difficult journey of trials and challenges. Imagine that at the end of your days you will be awaited by your ancestors, deceased loved ones, guides and teachers who will accompany you on the next stage of your journey. At least that is what many indigenous cultures believe, so perhaps you could take a moment to consider this reversed way of thinking. It will help you gain a new perspective on your life and opportunity here on Earth."

With that he got up, smiled and silently walked away, leaving me to quietly ponder his statement.

LessonThirteen
The Vase

On the table there was an exquisitely crafted vase with a delicate design of flowers and leaves. It seemed to be made of thin porcelain of the purest white. The outline was subtly curved and it held an arrangement of orange, white and yellow lilies. I was standing in the foyer of the school building, lost in thought and admiring the beauty of the bouquet in front of me, when I heard soft footsteps approaching behind me.

"Do you like it?" the Master asked and somehow I knew that it did not matter to him whether I did or did not, but that my answer did matter and that no matter what I said, there would be a lesson therein.

"It is exquisite," I said enthusiastically, before I had time to think my answer through. I had by now learned to reply in more than mere monosyllables, so I ventured forth to explain what I meant. "The colors of the design blend perfectly with the flowers in the vase, and the whole arrangement is very pleasing to the sight. The craftsmanship of the vase is quite unique and whoever made or designed it, was a person of refined taste and had a great appreciation for color and curve." I was quite pleased with my eloquent response and awaited what I thought were my due praises.

"Now look carefully at the vase," he responded after a moment of silence. "Tell me, has it altered in any way since you have sung its praises? Has that changed anything?" I thought for a moment and had to admit that it had not.

He continued with the lesson... "And if you had admonished it, finding fault with its texture and design, would that change anything, would it make it better? It is what it is and it has been made to be what it is. Our opinions about it will not change it. We can get as emotional about something as we want to, or, as is more often the case, as we do not want to, for most people are ruled by their emotions, even though they may wish this not to be so. That does not change the fact that tomorrow is another day and that the Earth takes 365 days to circumnavigate the sun." I looked up, ready to correct him, but stopped myself just in time.

"Yes, I know what you were going to say. You were going to say, 'except in leap year, when it takes 366 days' or perhaps you were going to say something closer to the truth, like, 'correction, it takes 365 and a quarter days for the earth to circumnavigate the sun.' When will you learn to deal in what is real and not in the fallacies and fantasies of man? For if you are going to correct me and add the quarter of a day, why not say more accurately, 'it takes the Earth 365 days and five hours to circumnavigate the sun'? Or give me the exact number of hours, minutes and seconds? That would be a valid correction indeed. But your ignorance has not permitted you to do so. Therefore you need to ask yourself the question: what in you wanted to correct me? For I would put forward that it was the desire to demonstrate your superior knowledge and show your educational superiority. But I deal in what is real and the Earth takes as long as it takes, whether we agree to it or not and whether we have an opinion about it or not.

I felt admonished and put in my place and for a moment silence fell between us. Then a question rose in me and I gave it a voice, "But what about humans? Do not humans need confirmation and appraisal? Do not your comments and reflections help me change?"

"Ah, yes," he replied. "The human is the great inventor of mirrors, forever seeking to see itself. It is rare for a human to want to know the truth, for mostly they want to see themselves in favorable light and do not take too well to criticism. Learn to value honest reflections, for they are harder to come by and more difficult to make; thus the person who gives them, as long as they are not emotionally biased, as in motivated by anger or jealousy or some such base emotion or governed by gain and loss, shows that they care and want to help. But very few people want and appreciate such help."

"I do," I said, knowing that I had been in receipt of such help and reflections from the very first moment when our exchanges began.

"I believe you do," he replied and then added after a moment, "but even you who want to improve and change, even you cannot stop the negative emotions of disappointment, regret and a wounded ego from rising when such reflections are offered to you. But never mind, the great recipe is to keep on going, for like this vase, you are what you are and nobody's opinion can change that. But with a little bit of self knowledge and outside help, you can make the small necessary adjustments to step on the path of development and improvement, whereby the aim is to get your life back and become the master and the student of you. Then you will become a student of everything that is real."

That last statement left me with many more questions, but he signaled me that our exchanges were over this day.

Lesson Fourteen
Beauty

I was looking at a cherry tree with many fruits, admiring the way the afternoon sun shone through the branches. It was warm and balmy and I paused for a moment, feeling pleased I was alive. Suddenly I heard the soft rustle of footsteps behind me and I turned around to once again face the Master as he walked towards me, leaning on his stick.

"What is beauty?" he asked. I thought about this for a moment and replied, "The sun, as it sets over the sea. Or a mountain range as the snowy peaks glisten in the rising sun. A starry night in the woods, a river as it reaches the sea, a swan as it majestically swims across a lake..." I was getting quite breathless by now and I realized that all my examples had one thing in common—they were all scenes from nature, unspoiled by human hand. I thought for a moment about beauty created by humans. "The Taj Mahal, the Egyptian pyramids, the Mona Lisa, the Sistine Chapel, Venice, Rome, Paris, Constantinople..." I said, and then I realized, no, they could not compare with Mother Nature. I felt I surely had the right answer this time. "Nature is beauty," I said, feeling satisfied with myself.

The Master laughed. He said, "Sunsets are for planets. To find out about human beauty, ask someone who cannot dance." I looked surprised and the Master confirmed, as he no doubt noticed my confusion, "I mean it. Find someone in a wheelchair and ask them what they consider beautiful," he said.

I set out early the next morning and drove to the nearest town. There I parked the car at the busy shopping area and it did not take me long before I spotted a man in a wheelchair, wheeling himself along through the streets of the downtown district. I stopped in front of him and asked him, "Can I please ask you a question?" The man nodded, though he looked somewhat surprised. "I want to know what true beauty is."

He looked up at me and paused. His eyes then took on a faraway look and he replied, "The ability to walk," he said and a tear gathered in the corner of his eye. "I knew beauty once but I looked for it elsewhere. I traveled far and wide looking for new sights on which to feast my eyes. I looked for beauty in the faces of women whom I met on my way. But now I know where true beauty lies—it is to simply be able to move every muscle of my body. You are beauty yourself and yet you do not see it, because you look in the mirror and see only imperfection. I feel sad for you. You possess the most beautiful of all gifts—the ability to do—and yet you do not see it." He hesitated for a moment and then continued, "I look at people and see perfection in God's work. Everything works as it is meant to. And yet we humans are never satisfied, always looking to improve upon what nature has given us."

He fell quiet and seemed lost in wistful contemplation. I could see that he was no longer aware of my presence and clearly considered the matter closed and the conversation concluded, because he rested his arms on the wheels of his chair and continued on his way.

Lesson Fifteen
On Life's Camera

The next day I woke up wondering what new challenges the day would bring. It felt as if something new was about to happen and I couldn't wait to get out of bed and prepare myself for what was to come. As I did so, I registered that I had not felt like this since being a child. Even if nothing new were to unfold, I was already a winner, simply because of how I felt. It made me think of those days when I was getting ready for a date or a new job or a trip into foreign parts, feeling more alive and excited than on days when nothing unusual was being anticipated.

If only I could live my life with that degree of keenness and anticipation, if I could look forward to each new day, as if it were a gift, waiting to be unraveled and fulfilled—my days could be so much richer and effective. Already I felt inspiration at the possibility of making acquaintance with this new me—one that is not familiar, blasé or spoilt, but greets each new challenge with a freshness and enthusiasm that never wears out.

I smiled to myself as I looked in the mirror, trying to imagine that I was looking at someone important who has a mission and purpose in life. And then I noticed that, by contrast, I had not normally smiled at myself in the mirror and that perhaps I was prone to taking myself far too seriously, thus preventing myself from self discovery by assuming that I already knew me. So I looked at myself with interest, wondering who was the person who was looking back at me, with a twinkle in her eye, getting ready for a new adventure called life.

After all, her life was going to be short and already a large part of it had been used up, possibly even more than a third. So whatever was to follow would need to be intense if it was going to amount to anything significant. And suddenly I saw myself and my life as a canvas, waiting to be painted upon. Also, for the first time ever, I felt that I was in control, in the sense that I could actually choose what colors I wished to paint upon this great white expanse and that I could be who and what I wanted to be. I had never before experienced such a freedom, except perhaps when I graduated from school and had absolutely no obligations, except the need to decide what I wanted to do next. However, now there was no family pressure or the good advice offered by mentors and peers. I really felt that once again I was being presented with an opportunity to become who and what I wanted to be.

Off I went to breakfast in the large dining hall, still feeling cocooned in a bubble, ready at any moment to burst free. I sat down with my coffee and croissant, looking out at a grey, overcast day outside, but feeling positive and optimistic inside. I was pondering how I could possibly extend and prolong this feeling and bring it into the more unfortunate situations that awaited me on my return to so-called 'normality,' for I felt as if I could really cope with anything now and, however mistakenly, that I could be confronted by any news or difficult challenge and still retain my composure. I was attempting to appreciate the predicament in question from the vantage of a very long view and an understanding of the part that I could play in this screenplay called life, if I only held onto the importance of the aims I had set myself.

This is where I ran into difficulty, for I had not set myself an aim, a goal, a priority, and therefore, whenever I attempted to look into the future, I found it difficult to see beyond today, tomorrow, next week or next year. And it was exactly at this point that I saw the Master approach my table and pause, as he asked, "May I sit down?"

"Of course, please do."

He sat down, waited for a moment and then began: "You found the next lesson yourself; well done! The decisions you are about to make are going to be important, because without deciding what you want to do with your life, you would never find the next step. I will not always be around to guide you, so you need to become your own forager and trailblazer. However, I must warn you that whatever you decide today, you can only do so with the knowledge and intelligence that you have accumulated through your life so far. And once you have made that decision, new perspectives will come into focus and you will begin to see your journey with new eyes and new perceptions. That is why you need to be flexible and not bound tomorrow by the decisions you make today in a way that could be too dogmatic and fixed and thereby render you closed to new revelations. Make sure that you are prepared to exchange aim for aim, as you move forward, just as a traveler looks to the next town or village as his next destination, as he continues along the route he has mapped out for himself. In his search he is always prepared to linger in one place or detour to another, if he finds this to be to his advantage or to the expediency of his chosen course, or economic in promulgating his further journey, or effective in bringing about greater knowledge about that which lies ahead of him.

"You will soon be leaving here and when you rejoin your life, it will never be quite the same, for inside you there have been small but significant changes. You will never again become quite so self absorbed as you had been before you came here and whatever you decide to do, you will always know that you are part of a greater plan, within which it is up to you to choose whether you want to be in harmony with the natural worlds within and around you or whether you want to stay blinkered and limited to the view that you are alone, separate, unsupported, even unloved. At least from now on the decision will be yours, and even if you change nothing about your life, it will be because you had consciously decided to do so."

He paused again and then said, "In deciding what you want to do, make sure that you take into account your skills and talents, for that consideration will help you identify what mission you have come to planet Earth to fulfill." He paused again for a moment and must have noticed my questioning look, for he soon added, "Oh yes, you have come here for a reason and the more you understand the tools with which nature has equipped you, the better you will be able to decide now how best to fulfill your life's tasking."

I sat there for a moment and it was as if a voice exploded inside my head with an epiphany accompanied by joy—I suddenly understood that I was here to help others! A flood of memories came rushing back as I pictured my childhood and earlier years. I remembered being able to place a hand over a friend's bruise or aching joint and how satisfying it had been to ease the pain. Yes, I will devote my life to healing, I thought and for a moment it seemed possible and, in fact, imperative to do so. I believed there would be further help and understanding and that I would find those in need whom I would be able to help. It seemed that my future was being decided and that I was merely acknowledging and confirming what had already been written and agreed.

The Master looked at me and smiled, as if he could read my thoughts and approved of what was happening inside my head. "I will now leave you to your contemplation. You have much to do," he said.

I now understood that the gifts that I had received were there for a reason. Throughout my life there were instances of premonitions and clairvoyance—I used to have pictures flash into my mind that would later turn out to be either accurate renditions of the past or previews of the future. I never knew why this was happening to me but now I realized that this ability was given to me for one purpose only—to help others! Indeed, I had a lot to do and needed to find ways to turn my calling into a reality. It was one thing to know what needed to be done, another to find practical ways to do it.

"Remember to smile often," the Master said. "You are always on life's camera."

And with that he rose and slowly walked away.

Lesson Sixteen
Religious Moments

I had been summoned earlier that morning and was now sitting in front of the Master; he closed his eyes as he asked the question, "What is the most religious moment of your life?"

Religious? Me? What could he possibly mean? My mind went a-racing through the annals of my short history here on Earth. There seemed to be so few significant life-altering moments. As I searched harder, I began to see pictures emerging from my past—the day my niece was born and how my sister-in-law had explained to me that giving birth was the greatest feeling of fulfillment she had ever experienced. Then there was the summer's day at camp when my friend Angela fell into the river and was being swept away by the strong current. I had immediately called out for help, then jumped into the cold waters myself and held onto her for just long enough until an experienced swimmer came to our rescue. I believe my quick response had saved my friend from drowning and I remember well the feeling of holding onto her as she was struggling for her life in the deep, cool waters of the mountain stream. Then there was the inspiration and satisfaction I felt when I first saw my name in print, having written a report from the annual Easter parade for the local paper. Somehow these, although important to me, did not seem to rank as religious. I had to ask myself the question—what does he mean by religion? And then, suddenly, I got a picture of my life as being part of a process—coming from somewhere and going somewhere, here briefly and gone tomorrow. This flash of insight was almost blinding and I was sure I had the right answer, "My most religious moment must be the moment I was born, the time of entry and beginning," I replied, feeling rather pleased with myself.

He looked at me and in his eyes I saw something that was akin to pity and I knew yet again that there was more to learn.

"Ah," he said, this time his face resuming the composure of tranquility and omniscience, "this is a trick question. If you do not say 'now,' you are either mentally living in the past, which is fixed, gone and unchangeable, or in the future, which is vague, uncertain and not yet here. Only this moment can really be religious because it is only the now that offers the opportunity for change."

The lesson might have been over, but it was certainly not over for me. I suddenly was realizing the value of the present and seeing how I was forever chasing the next stimulation and the next excitement, ambition or duty. I could even remember catching myself out one day when waiting for an elevator, on my way up to see a friend in her fifth floor apartment. As I waited for the elevator my impatient brain kept producing images of an elevator arriving at the ground floor, opening up and taking me to my destination. Then, as soon as the projected image became a reality, the picture changed as I entered the elevator—now I was picturing how I remembered the fifth floor corridor to look like. And then again, as soon as the image was framed as reality within the opening door of the elevator, I pictured the door of my friend's apartment, as I looked for the number of her apartment on both sides of the corridor. It was at that moment that I had realized that I was always projecting into the future. And then for a brief while I even noticed that while I was talking with my friend, in my head I was already planning what I was going to cook for dinner and reviewing other chores I had to do by the end of the week. This revelation lasted for a short while, and I soon reverted to my usual habits forgetting about the extra insight that for some reason was afforded me that day. The incident was soon altogether forgotten until this day...

He looked at me inquisitively and it seemed that he understood where I had just visited within the chambers of my memory.

"This is a very important lesson for you to remember. Your now is sacred, for within it you can change, alter and take control of your destiny. It will also shape your future and explain your past," he added and I felt that something important had irrevocably altered within my view of myself and life.

Lesson Seventeen
I Don't Like You

I was standing by the mirror in my little room, examining my face and trying to look at it, as if it belonged to another person and not to me. 'Is she attractive?' I asked myself. 'Do I like her?' I inclined my head from side to side, trying to look at my face from different angles.

The Master suddenly walked into the room—quietly and gently, following a soft, hardly audible knock on the door. With little warning he walked decisively into the middle of the room, while I turned around to meet him, expectant and no doubt with an enquiring look in my eyes. He waited silently for a moment and as we stood opposite each other there was a short delay, while he seemed to wait for me to compose and still myself, as I got over the initial shock of seeing him in my room, so close and so directly in front of me. Then he said, perfectly calmly and without emotion, "I don't like you."

When he had satisfied himself that his words had registered with me and that I did not know what to do with them or how to respond, he simply turned around and left the room. I was left standing there, feeling confused, bewildered, unsure of anything any more. He doesn't like me, I kept saying to myself in my head, trying desperately to understand the significance of that statement. But try as hard as I might, I couldn't work it out and all I felt was a mounting dejection, rejection and loneliness. Slowly more and more my feelings took over my thinking and I felt that I began to like myself less and less as well.

Finally, I brought myself into such a state that all I could do was sit on the bed and stare out the window, feeling that even nature—the trees, the birds, the flowers and the butterflies—didn't like me any more, though I could not notice any change in their behavior patterns at all—the trees were still swaying as they yielded to the pressure of the wind, and the butterflies flitted from flower to flower in their pursuit of nutriment.

Several hours passed as I sank deeper and deeper into depression. My inability to think straight was quite paralyzing and devastating. I went from defiance to anger and back to depression again, all the time trying to convince myself that I really didn't care what other people thought about me. One thing became clear from those few dark hours and that was that despite all my protestations, I really did care very much.

Finally, around six o'clock, as the sun was lowering towards the horizon and the light in the room softened and I was still rooted to my spot on the bed, the door opened and the Master was back. He pulled up a chair, sat down in front of me and quietly said, "I did not lie when I said I didn't like you, but I did not speak for myself. Somewhere in the world there is someone who does not like you—I spoke on their behalf. Personally, I neither like nor dislike you. I am simply here to help you, because you called out for help. That is my function, that is my job.

"Realize that there is no one in the whole wide world whom everybody likes. There will always be those who don't like you for whatever reason. You must learn not to mind and above all to like yourself enough so that no one and nothing can undermine that relationship you have built with yourself. So you must begin now, if you are to be anything at all in this life and in these times, if you are to build a good, healthy, progressive relationship with yourself that can withstand verbal attacks, the breakdown of relationships, false or truthful accusations, disappointments, failures and a consistent lack of success. You are the only friend you will ever have that has accompanied you right through your entire life and will surely be there at the end. You must foster your self-respect, your confidence and your belief in yourself by fulfilling your promises to yourself and giving yourself the benefit of the doubt.

"Something powerful believed in you enough to give you life and sustain you so far. I believe in you so that you might have the will and fortitude to believe in yourself. You are, after all, a representative of the human race and therefore you have all the equipment you need to succeed."

He paused for a moment and added, "I will leave you now so that you may contemplate your future and your renewed relationship with yourself." With these words he quietly stood up, put the chair back to where it was before he had entered and walked out the door, closing it silently behind him.

Lesson Eighteen
Joining In

I was sitting on the terrace outside the dining room in the increasing twilight, sipping a cup of coffee and watching groups of people at other tables. Some were talking, others were drinking their afternoon tea and still others were sitting in silence, either absorbed by the scenery that stretched out in front of them or writing notes which I assumed were to do with their experiences of the day or, like myself, they were watching all the other people on the terrace.

My eyes were particularly caught by a group of three women who were sitting around a table in close proximity to each other, obviously enjoying each other's company and conversation. They were talking quite animatedly and at regular interludes I could hear bursts of rich, deep laughter, the kind that comes from the joy of a shared story, joke or repartis.

I was sitting there thinking that I, too, would like to be part of a close and intimate exchange, that I longed for companionship and that this group of women would probably be accessible and open to having a stranger join them. I felt curious, because up till now I had not had any conversations with the other course participants outside of the training and I felt it was time to socialize and discover what the others were up to. I wondered who these other people were and how did they come to be here.

Just as I was about to rise and move towards the table which was located at the west end of the terrace, the Master appeared, as if from nowhere and sat down beside me. No questions asked, simply there he was and I felt I knew there was a new lesson to come. I immediately let go of my plans, both mentally and emotionally and turned to him, silently and expectantly, waiting for him to speak. I did not have to wait long.

"I know you intend to join that group of women," he said, subtly pointing with his entire hand in their direction. "I would advise against it. The reason they are getting on so well together is because they have just recently had an intense experience together and they are talking about it, comparing notes and sharing their stories. It took three months of their working together to build the trust and openness between them within which they can have such a candid and frank conversation. If you were to join them now, because of their open and compassionate state, they would be glad to have you in their midst, but it would make a further exploration of their newly acquired insights quite impossible. You would change their mental and emotional state simply by being there and this would completely alter the situation, even if you were to say nothing.

"So, realize that when you join a group of people, or even one other person, you bring your state, condition, thoughts, experiences, history, desires, ambitions, opinions, prejudices and much, much more to that situation, thus inevitably and irrevocably changing it. You might think you would like to be included into their intimacy, but you need to know that you would have destroyed the very thing you wish to partake of by attempting to do so.

"You see, people approach situations from their own personal standpoint, trying to see what is in it for them, what they can take or gain from each encounter or exchange. To be sensitive and helpful to others means to understand them, to adopt, at least temporarily, their viewpoint and to ask oneself the question, whether one is adding to, enhancing and supporting the current happening or perhaps working against it. In other words, what would you bring to those three women as a gift, as an offering to promote their well-being as well as your own, or were you only thinking of yourself and what you could have gained from them and their previously worked for ease?"

He stopped me before I could say anything. "No, don't answer that. It is for you to consider and think about; it is certainly no concern of mine. I am here to offer you alternative views and to help you to expand your thinking so that you may include others, your environment and eventually the universe as well into your daily and habitual deliberations.

"Here is another consideration. Each of those three women is different and each contributes something unique and individual to their exchange. Two are very bright, light-hearted and settled in their life. The third is somewhat frustrated, serious, quick to anger and lacks a sense of humor. In their coming together today there has had to be a lot of give and take, tolerance and acceptance, for the two who have been friends for several years to share their stories and their humor with the third. However, the third thinks that in this conversation she is an equal partner and is currently under the false impression that she, too, is capable of having such a colorful exchange and will be looking for it in her future dealings with others, forever being disappointed and disillusioned, wondering why it is not happening to her. Until one day she might realize that this experience she is now having was not of her own making.

"Thus, learn to generate intimacy and well-being for yourself, so you can then pass it on to others and thus draw them to yourself by your cheerful radiation and sunny disposition. Otherwise you will always be reliant on the work of others and will forever be looking to them to see where your next learning or entertainment is coming from."

And with that he rose silently and walked off as quietly as he came, as if he had never really been there and it felt to me as if I had been dreaming. I looked up and saw that the three women at the western table had gone too, leaving their coffee cups and napkins behind them. Even if they had still been there, I now knew that I would not have been able to join them at this time.

Lesson Nineteen
What's In a Name?

I was sitting in the library, not because I wanted to read, but because I wanted to be quiet. I had looked around and read some of the titles on the shelves that were built into all four walls of the room. There were many books which I recognized—the religious books of the world, books exploring traditional thought, philosophy, the classics—and many which I did not recognize—books written by authors with exotic, foreign sounding names, old volumes that must have been produced decades ago, and even centuries ago.

Old books have a familiar, dusty smell which I knew well from the antique shops and old book dealers I used to enjoy frequenting. It made me feel secure and at home, knowing that even here a book is still a book and that the Bible, The Koran, the Upanishads were all frequently read and referred to.

I sat down at a small table with a reader's lamp upon it and pulled out my diary from the bag I had brought with me. I didn't quite know what I was going to write, but I felt an urgent need to record some of my thoughts and feelings, because as each new day and one set of registrations was superimposed by the next, I needed to try to catch the moment and seize the opportunity of recording it for my future; otherwise these new understandings and perceptions would be lost forever.

The date—now what was it? I couldn't remember exactly and I was no longer even sure what day of the week it was. I looked around for clues, but saw no calendar on the walls and I was no longer clear whether I had been there for three, five, or even seven days. Time seemed to have slowed down or speeded up, or both at once; I was not sure. But it felt as if a year had gone by already, so much had happened, but here I was, still in the midst of this unusual learning experience, uncertain whether it would end tomorrow or the next day, or perhaps even next week.

I needed to gather my thoughts, slow down and try to work out what was actually going on. I had arrived on a Tuesday, or was it Wednesday? Then there were how many lessons and days and encounters? No matter how hard I tried to work it out, the facts evaded me and I couldn't quite find a point of certainty from which to begin. My world was no longer measured and ordered according to dates, schedules and deadlines; I seemed to be in the midst of a topsy-turvy existence and I didn't mind; I didn't mind at all.

And then I remembered the Master's words during our first interview when he had mentioned that time here was different and could not be measured in ordinary ways. So where was I and what was really going on? Was I held here as hostage? No, he had also said that I could leave at any time. However, one thing I knew for certain—I did not want to.

So I paused for a moment, wondering what the next lesson would be, when I noticed an envelope with my name on it, resting against the base of the lamp on the table where I was sitting. I don't know how I could not have seen it there before. I picked it up and opened it. It was a brief note, typewritten on a single sheet of paper. "There will be no lesson today, but there is a task for you to fulfill before we meet again. Write down on a piece of paper your name as well as all the nicknames different people have called you by as far as you can remember. Then take each name—your first name, your parents' name, your married name and all of your nicknames that you can remember and write down what each one means or has meant to those who have known you. Be as detailed as you can. You have the entire afternoon to do this."

This seemed like a difficult task, because it entailed going into my history, but I was eager to try it. I started with my current name—

Barbara Johnson—and wrote it down in full, at the same time realizing that not many people would use that particular variation of my name and if they did, they were probably people who dealt with me on a professional basis, not friends or family, but rather associates, doctors, lawyers, accountants... They had one view of me and I could quite easily imagine what that would be like—superficial, surface views based upon my behavior, appearance, age, looks and financial status. It was, however, a very interesting and revealing exercise, for it caused me to view myself from outside of myself. which, I had to admit, I had never done before.

Then came the various nicknames and diminutive versions of my Christian name and the various attitudes, which people had displayed towards me through the years. How did they view me? There were certainly clues in their language, intonation, in the frequency of their dealing with me, in the warmth, demands of me, generosity towards me. I was unexpectedly seeing much more than I had ever done before and I was beginning to find the exercise very revealing indeed. My pen was moving faster as I was covering more and more pages of the writing pad that was lying on the desk in front of me.

Then there were other epithets, bad names, qualities attributed to me, pet names, accusations, praises. Slowly I moved backwards in time towards adolescence and childhood, where I raked out from oblivion multiple nicknames that were implemented by my teachers, parents, brother, friends and classmates for multiple reasons and on numerous occasions, with an entire scale of accompanying endearments or animosities. I will not mention these here, but some of them came to see the light of day after several years of obscurity and anonymity. For example, I remembered a boy in high school who used to call me The Plague simply because I would not date him.

By dinnertime I was finished and quite exhausted, for I felt I had been on a journey through my history, attempting to find my identity, that elusive me that others knew well but I might not have even suspected its existence. Then, the final part to this exercise, although not requested, seemed to automatically present itself to me: I was trying, like in a jigsaw puzzle, to bring the pieces together and establish who and what I was to whom. I was surprised at the range and variety of portraits that was emerging from this attempt and in putting the image together I was getting more lost, rather than more found. But some new realizations were also appearing—above all the picture of names that were conspicuously absent; I began to see with some degree of surety what I was definitely not.

As I was pondering these issues over the evening meal, Mrs. Pearce came to my table and passed on the message that the Master would like to see me in the Pink Room after I had finished. I pulled out my notes and had a final perusal before I ventured towards the interview room—I wanted to make sure that I had the results of the exercise clear in my mind before I confronted him.

He was sitting at the table reading as I entered. He looked up and pointed to a chair beside him. I came in, sat down, with notes in hand, looking at him expectantly. It was not long before he began to speak, "I don't need to know what you have written down this afternoon," he said, laying his hands on his knees as he spoke. For the first time I noticed that his hands were rather large and firm, with long, tapered fingers.

"This exercise is for you and you alone. It is devised to give you an insight into what kind of appeal, indifference or allergenic reaction you have caused over the years in others, so that you can see yourself through the prism of multiple eyes—none of these images complete or correct, because everyone, even I, will see you through the perspective of their own particular biases, experiences, understandings, misunderstandings, allergies, likes and dislikes. But hopefully you can begin to see yourself both from outside as well as inside, which is the key to comprehending your part in a greater reality, which is small, as well as your potential therein, which is large. You must begin to not take yourself so seriously, to not be so terribly preoccupied with your own predicaments and to see yourself within the context of everything around you, otherwise you will never be able to reach out to others with true compassion and effective help."

I wanted to protest when he spoke about being 'terribly preoccupied with my own predicament' but I had to realize that before coming here, that is all I had thought about for almost an entire day! I also remembered the afternoon I spent worrying about the fact that he might not have liked me. It made me smile at my previous foolishness.

"Is there anything you want to ask or say to me?" he asked, after a moment of silence, during which I realized he had clearly finished.

"Yes. What caught me the most in doing this exercise is the realization that there are certain names that are not on this list. For example, no one has ever called me mean, petty or a thief, to mention a few obvious examples. To me that part of the tasking was reassuring, for if I ever feel inclined to call myself by such names, I will now remember that no one else has ever done so, so why should I?"`

"Good. It is beginning to work. Do not think the exercise is completed—it will continue for as long as you are alive. You are getting ready to begin in earnest, for the most important foundation to any real knowledge is the imperative, 'know thyself.'"

"There is one further aspect of this that I would like to share with you," I said. "In looking through my notes, I see there is a thread running through them and that something that almost all have always said to me was that I keep on trying. I seem to have a persistence that is visible and recognizable to others. I have never quite appreciated this quality in myself until now, so in view of this I have found myself pulling on this thread and, like the native peoples of this land, I wish to take on a new name—I intend to call myself Try—not externally, but for myself and for when I think and deliberate upon these matters."

"Very well, Try. I shall call you by that name as well. I will see you tomorrow, Try. Good night, Try."

And with that threefold reference to my name, the interview was complete. I got up and walked quietly towards the door, as the Master returned to his reading.

Lesson Twenty
Choice

It was another warm, sunny day and I was having my afternoon coffee on the terrace, when Mrs. Pearce came up to the table with a large plate of cookies and sweets.

"Some of the girls have made some treats. I'll leave them here for you to choose from." And before I had time to say anything, she was off again, having left the large platter behind, no doubt in order to give me time to make my selection in peace and solitude. I turned my attention to the variety of goodies in front of me: some I recognized and some I did not. There were pieces of fudge, chocolate treats, caramel mousse in small dishes, sesame bars, fruit tarts, what looked like peanut cookies, brownies and several other assorted desserts, all tastefully arranged in co-centric circles around a central core. It was very difficult to make a choice, especially as the mixture of aromas reached my nostrils and my appetite was accelerated into a noisy demand. I was still hesitating when I heard quiet footsteps approach the table and I suddenly saw the Master standing in front of me, smiling encouragingly.

"Have you made up your mind yet?" he asked, as if there had been a time limit set or this was a tasking that I had urgently needed to fulfill.

"No. They all look so delicious..."

"How much energy have you used up so far making your choice?" he asked, as he interrupted my train of thought.

He sat down opposite me at the small table and I knew that the next exchange had already begun. I thought about his question for a brief moment and I had to admit, "Too much."

"Yes. And whatever your choice, you would immediately wonder that perhaps it would have been better if you had made a different decision."

I smiled. He was right.

"Perhaps even leading to overeating or overindulgence," he continued and I instinctively knew he was not talking about the cookies any more and that there was more about this lesson to come.

"Sometimes, to preserve energy and avoid anxiety, it is best to make a choice and abide by it, until there is enough information to make a correction. Sometimes it is far better to make a decision and learn from the experience, even if it is a faulty one, than not to decide at all."

I could see his point. There was a short pause and then he added, "Sometimes, in order to help another person preserve energy and save time, both of which are the most valuable commodities a person can possess, you can nudge them towards a decision, especially in unimportant matters. I must warn you, though—I would never influence another person in life-changing decisions, for they will always blame you if it goes wrong. Every human should have the privilege and right to make their own decisions and to learn from the outcome of their actions. All you can do to help is to be there for them, to support them in their struggles and to offer any information that they might need and you might have to give. You can support their endeavor and offer your personal experience or your personal preference. If you say, 'If I were you, I would never go out with that man,' as an example, they can never turn around and accuse you of ruining their life. Better still, use an analogy or personal story to illustrate your mindset or preference, rather than trying to influence theirs. On the other hand, if you do recommend a course of action that the person consequently fails to take, they will always feel awkward with you and in all probability you will lose a friend.

"But back to unimportant decisions that use up a lot of energy: I recommend you try the wafer thin chocolate biscuit with the mint topping." He smiled as I obediently reached for the cookie, relieved that indeed, a decision had been made at last. At the same time I consciously considered that I was prepared to trust him in this small decision, but that important matters would need to be settled by me and me alone, using all available tools, like my conscience, my instinct and my experience. I smiled as I bit into the wafer. It was, indeed, delicious.

He smiled back, got up from his chair and said before he departed, "I think you've got it. You trusted the information I was able to share with you but you were the one who made the decision and I see you have taken the responsibility for the outcome of your choice. For myself, I am glad you like it."

Lesson Twenty-One
Fire

We were sitting in the small interview room and I had been informed that this was to be my last conversation in the series of twenty-one exchanges. I already felt sad about leaving and was hoping that I might be able to return some day.

"Isn't it amazing how a fire can seem dead, but when you poke it, a few sparks appear and then perhaps a flame and finally the fire is re-awoken and brought back to life and from that moment on, as long as it is regularly fed and stoked, it can burn brightly for a very long time, warming all those who come into contact with it, offering warmth and life, inspiration and contagion?" the Master said. "You are no different and you need poking and challenging and stimulating; you need tests and surprises and new adventures. Life will provide these for you, but you must learn to stoke your own fire, for only you will know where the line lies between complacency and initiative, between laziness and challenge, between compliance and risk, between habit and daring.

"So never settle to who you already think you are—you are far more, far better than you ever thought possible. And you will only discover this if you learn to be your own teacher and mentor. How do you do this, you ask. By not settling for what you have already achieved, by demanding more and by asking yourself challenging questions, such as, 'Who am I?', 'What do I want?', 'Where am I going?' and above all, 'Why?', 'Why?', 'Why?'

"If you have a clearly defined goal, whatever it may be, everything you meet, every new situation will either support it or take away from it. Thus from the platform of knowing what you want, you will find it so much easier to make decisions in life, both large and small; it doesn't matter. But beware, because every decision you make about what you want will have its consequences and by its very nature, it will exclude all else that does not fit with it. Thus be careful that in deciding what you do want you do not exclude that which you also want but which is incompatible with your first want. Thus you also need to make a list of priorities so that in the case of conflicting wants, you will always know how to choose.

"If you do this, you will no longer waste so much of your energy and time on hesitation, not knowing, wavering and all those uncertainties that have plagued you and eaten up the time that could have been so usefully utilized elsewhere.

"So my final advice to you is contained in the words 'know thyself' with the added codisil—keep questioning who and what you are because as you grow and change, so will your desires, priorities and needs. Treat every day as if it were your first and your last—in fact, your only chance to learn, to be, to do. For that is the truth— your time is now and it will always be now. Then all those nows will finally add up to become your own unique work of art—your life.

"Try to implement these lessons and remember who you are. I will be with you in spirit, along with many unseen friends who want you to succeed. If you call on us, we will be there in support, guiding you towards the next success or challenge. Believe in you and you will cause the world to believe in you as well. And if you adhere to your purpose well, we will meet again when it is time for you to engage in the next level of training."

He looked at me with his penetrating dark eyes and added, before I had a chance to speak, "Thanks are not necessary. I know you are grateful and you appreciate the lessons you have leaarned. So go back into your life and make the world a better place." He smiled and I smiled back. I felt no more words were necessary.

Part Three

Back to Reality

Chapter One
On the Way Back

So that was it. Twenty-one lessons and the training was over. I did not want to go. I was feeling so at home and alive, I wanted it to continue. But I needed to go back into the world of everyday living and pass a test, though I had no idea what this test was supposed to be and how I would recognize it. Or perhaps there would be several tests. How long would that take and what would be expected of me? I didn't have a clue.

I was still no longer sure how much time had passed since I had first arrived, but as I was certain that at no time were there more than two lessons in any one day, I was convinced that it had to be much more than one week since the lessons began. I tried to work it out in my mind, but I kept losing count and I found that I could not remember all twenty-one instructions. So I gave up and decided to check out the date as soon as I arrived in town.

I walked slowly back to the room that had hosted me these past days and nights and as I packed my bag, my mind started to turn towards what lay ahead. It all seemed very unreal and distant somehow, almost as if it existed in some other dimension, on some other plane. I walked towards the car and noticed, as I did so, that there were very few other cars in the parking lot in front of the main building and I did not see any people milling around, either. I got in my car and slowly drove away, continuously looking in my rear view mirror at the grand old building that was receding behind me. And then, there I was, in front of the gates which automatically opened as soon as I approached them—I felt as if someone had been watching me and was anticipating my departure.

As I drove down the lane towards the main road, I passed the bus stop which had been the subject of one of the lessons. I then turned the corner, heading back towards town and I noticed that mists were gathering in front of me and this brought to mind the day I had arrived. I drove into the fog and as I did so, visibility worsened, until I was driving under ten miles an hour, trying hard to keep close to the bright yellow line that ran down the middle of the road. Slowly, slowly I continued to make progress, until it felt as if I had been driving for a very long time. My eyes were strained and my posture felt very uncomfortable, as I tried to peer ahead, looking out of the front windscreen. As I began to worry that perhaps I had inadvertently taken a wrong turning and that really I was hopelessly lost, suddenly the mists cleared and I was approaching the main road. There it was in front of me, in full view, clear and sunlit, with not a trace of fog on the ground or cloud in the sky.

With relief, I turned onto the main road, which was still only a country highway with not much traffic to show for it. As I did so, I felt a change, as if some of the enchantment of the past days had vanished and I was on my way to so-called 'normality' again, whatever that really meant. However, I also felt that there had been changes that had gone on in me and that really I was no longer the same person that had driven this way in the opposite direction all those days ago.

As I drove towards the town, in the light of the setting sun, I realized I was going home and that soon I would need to confront the situation I had left behind. It all began to come back to me and I remembered with much greater clarity that there were decisions to make and situations to be resolved. And as the first houses of the town were becoming visible on either side of the road, I realized that there was no longer any hesitation in me; and this was where I could best sense the change that had occurred in me. For it was obvious and simple and straightforward and required no further deliberations on my part: all I wanted was the truth and honesty and a real life, so the only thing left for me to do was to confront the situation head on and take it from there. If it meant the end of a relationship and the need to start again, so be it. I could not and would not live a lie. Not any more. The deception had to end and I needed to start putting in place real, concrete foundations for my future to be built upon in firmness and with a lasting formation.

Thus with resolve and determination I approached the first shops, as I headed towards the town center. I stopped the car in front of a convenience store and went in to buy a newspaper, so that I could reconnect to reality and what was going on in the world, as well as buy myself a drink. I picked up a bottle of spring water and a newspaper from the rack and brought both items over to the cash desk. I handed the cashier a five dollar bill and as I waited for my change, I glanced at the newspaper and, noticing the date, exclaimed, "Oh, sorry, I've got an old paper here. I'll go back to get today's" The woman behind the till paused with the change in hand, turned the paper towards her, read the date and replied, "No, that's today's paper, all right. The twenty-first of October, Friday. That's today."

"Are you sure? Today is the twenty-first of October? It can't be." I was incredulous.

"But it is." She sounded definite. As she handed me the change, she must have noticed the look of disbelief still lingering on my face, for she addressed the man who now stood behind me waiting for his turn in the queue, "Sir, could you please tell this lady what date it is? She doesn't seem to believe me."

I put the change in my wallet, picked up the newspaper and bottle of water and, feeling, embarrassed, I now turned to face the man behind me, who replied, "Certainly. It's the twenty-first of October, Friday. And tomorrow will be Saturday, the twenty-second of October. And yesterday was Thursday, the twentieth of October."

"Thank you," I replied and looking at the woman behind the counter, I added, "I believe you," and with that, I turned to walk towards the door.

My mind was racing, for I could not understand what had happened. How could it still be the same day I had left, when I had spent so many days at the Human Development Center? Unless it had all been a dream, of course. But then I knew it was not, for I felt different and changed. This was very confusing indeed.

I walked slowly to the car and, looking at the headlines of the leading articles in the paper, it was confirmed that the stories were familiar and the faces were the same as those that appeared on the television news the night before I had gone on that fateful trip to the cleaners and consequently on the human development course. So what had happened? I knew it was real. I could not give up the notion that it had really happened. And then I remembered the Master warning that time there was different and that it passed so much faster at the Human Development Center. I also vaguely remembered fairy tales from my childhood in which time would become elastic and a person would go missing for a month or maybe even a year, but only an hour or a day would have gone by in the mundane world. Perhaps this is what they meant; perhaps the world of enchantment lived on, only now it dressed itself up in different disguises, as the world of fairies, goblins and dwarves had long been discredited and even children did not believe in them any more.

Here my knowledge of legends and ancient lore ran out and I could not recall hearing any modern day story about people being lost in time and returning to tell the tale. But then I had never studied the subject, having dismissed all fairy tales as fiction and bogus. So there I was, without preconception or foreknowledge—slightly bewildered and very curious, like someone waking up from a deep sleep and wondering where they are. Everything looked slightly different and although nothing seemed to have changed on the outside, how I viewed it had altered. There was a certain detachment in my demeanor and even this new state of affairs was not affecting me as I suspect it would have under earlier circumstances.

I drove on towards the house, considering that if it really was the date that appeared on the newspaper, then my note and subsequent disappearance would have not been noticed by anyone yet and therefore I would not need to explain myself to anyone. I drew comfort from this fact as I drove on. I also noticed that I no longer felt angry at anyone—Andrew or Anne—or hurt or disappointed. I simply wanted to now get on with my life, whatever that would turn out to be.

As I drove into the driveway of the suburban house we lived in, the last vestiges of light were gradually disappearing from the evening sky and all the streetlights were now blazing in the twilight, forming pools of light and creating shadows just beyond their reach. I was home again, though I was no longer sure whether this particular house would continue to be my home for much longer.

Chapter Two
The Confrontation

I walked into the house, trying to remember what else had happened this day and trying to piece the sequence of events together in my mind, so that I could think of it as one colloidal time continuum, where one event and one moment blends into the next, and the next, and the next.

As I walked through the door and closed it behind me, I noticed my note, still there where I had left it on the hall table, intact, unread, untouched. I picked it up and proceeded to tear it up, still marveling at the trick time was playing on me. And just as I began to wonder whether I should phone Andrew at the office, I noticed the beeping phone message machine and pressed the button to check the incoming calls. The first was a brief hello from my mother, the second was a reminder from my dentist that it was time for a check-up, and finally there was a call from Andrew.

"Honey, I've got to go out for dinner with a client tonight. If you want to come along, please call the office by six." I looked at my watch—it was five to six. I dialed the company's number and got through to the automatic answering service—obviously Anita had already gone home. I pressed Andrew's extension and got his voice mail; he must have gone as well.

I went upstairs and started to run a bath; I suddenly felt tired and lonely. Everything around me looked familiar but felt alien, as if I no longer belonged to this world of pretence, make-belief and sham friends. As the water was running, I looked at myself in the mirror and was reminded of the lesson on beauty and on being on life's camera. I smiled and looked at myself as I had probably never looked before—with understanding and compassion, but without personal involvement, as if I were looking at somebody else. Every moment needed its fulfillment and I was beginning to feel, once again, that exciting feeling of being really alive, and the knowing that anything can happen at any time.

I was pulled back from my thought process abruptly, as I could hear the door slam—someone had just walked in the front door. I was not yet prepared for a confrontation and I also could not understand who it could be, so I called out, opening the door to the bathroom and leaning over the stair railing:

"Andy, is that you?"

"Yes, it's me. I've just dropped in to change." Before I knew it, he was coming up the stairs and the voice was getting louder.

"Hi, honey, had a good day?" he asked as he came up onto the landing and a moment later he was kissing me on the cheek. He wasn't really looking at me, but headed straight for the bathroom, where I could hear him start the shower. He soon came out and went into the bedroom, pulling his tie off as he did so. I went into the bathroom and turned the bath water off.

"I need to talk to you," I said, following him into the bedroom. The closet doors were open and he was beginning to pull out a change of clothes for the evening.

"Sure, but not now, honey. I need to go or I'll be late. Are you coming?" he looked at me, obviously ascertaining whether I was dressed for dinner or not. Clearly I was not. As I saw his eyes glance over me, I felt as if I could read his thoughts.

"I guess not," he said with a finality as if he were saying, 'well, that's that.'

"How about when you get back?"

"Sure, but you know what it's like. I'll probably be very tired and I do have an important presentation tomorrow."

"But it is important," I protested. Then I added, "I'll wait up for you."

"All right, but I can't guarantee what time that will be," he said as he headed back into the bathroom.

I hesitated. Perhaps I should go with him; that way I could at least talk with him on the way. But then I would have to listen to his co-workers talk over dinner about insurance and figures and financing... no, I needed to stay home and think.

When he came out again he was dressed and ready to go.

"All right, I'm off. See you later." A peck on the cheek and he was walking down the stairs, putting on his jacket as he went.

So I had time to think about it. I made myself a cup of tea and sat down in my favorite armchair where I could think best. I found that the past three years were parading before my eyes in picture form— the endless dinners, outings and entertainment, mostly for prospective customers. The talk of contracts and terms, the search for the next deal. I looked hard and from the place where I now could examine my situation, I saw my life to be empty and flat and going nowhere. I could see the years flowing by and I realized how short life really is. What was it going to amount to if I let it simply drift on? Andrew was a decent man by social standards, but neither he nor I up to this point had any clearly defined goals, except to get by and survive, with some easement and luxury and pleasure thrown in. I wanted more and I wanted my life to amount to something. I wanted to be able to look back at the years with pride and the satisfaction of accomplishment, and not be subject to regrets or unfulfilled hopes. Every year I was growing older and it became clear to me that I needed to make up my mind now what I could do and how I wanted to do it.

I had fallen asleep in the chair. I was suddenly awoken by the door banging shut. In walked Andrew looking tired, spent, older. He was carrying his jacket over his shoulder and he threw it onto the sofa as soon as he walked in.

"I'm tired," he said as he sat down, stretching his legs and pushing off his shoes alternatively with the other foot.

"How did it go?" I enquired. His eyes were closed by now as he rested his head against the back of the sofa.

"It was all right. I won't know if they'll buy or not till next week."

I felt sorry for him; he looked so vulnerable and tired.

"I know we were going to talk. But you look so tired. Perhaps it can wait till tomorrow. You're not going anywhere tomorrow, are you?"

"I told you I have an important presentation tomorrow afternoon. And before that I have a lunchtime meeting with the boss. It was the only time he could make it," he said slowly. "But I'll be here in the morning."

"All right, let's wait till then. Do you want a coffee?" He looked as if he could do with one.

"That would be great. Thanks." And that was the end of that. At least for that day.

I woke up early, urgent about the day. I got up and prepared everything for breakfast. Today was the day my new life would begin —I knew it. As soon as Andrew arrived at the kitchen table, I poured him a cup of coffee and sat down opposite him. Hardly a word had been spoken, except 'morning' and 'coffee,' when finally I came out with it, "I know you are having an affair with Anne."

Just as I thought he would, he looked surprised, even shocked.

"An affair with Anne?" he repeated incredulously. "What are you talking about?"

He's stalling for time, I thought and hastened to explain, so as not to lose the advantage of the surprise, "Yes, I found the receipt from the Golden Dusk hotel in your jacket pocket."

He was still not comprehending, or perhaps he was simply pretending well.

"Golden Dusk hotel? I've never heard of it." He sounded very convincing.

"Andrew, I've got the receipt. It has your name on it."

"That's impossible. I've never been there. Show me."

I pulled it out of the kitchen drawer, where I had hidden it under the cutlery caddy.

"Here. Here's the proof." My heart was pounding now. How could he deny it any longer? He examined it thoroughly in silence. Then he said, slowly enunciating his words, "It does have my name on it. And it is my Visa expense card. But I wasn't there. What's the date? September sixth... Where was I then? I can't remember."

"I can help you there. You were supposed to be at a sales conference. At least that's what you told me."

"That's right. I remember now. John was meeting up with Anne somewhere at a hotel and he had forgotten to bring his card, so I let him use mine. That's all. You can ask him to confirm it."

He handed the offending bill back to me. "He's paid me back," he added with obvious satisfaction.

I sat back down at the table, crestfallen. I didn't know what to say. All those doubts and worries, all for nothing. I couldn't believe it. It was too easy. But it did all add up. I remembered that the bellboy recognized Anne from the photograph, but not Andrew.

"And I had you tried, sentenced and convicted, all without the privilege of an attorney."

Andrew smiled one of his disarming smiles, obviously feeling satisfied with himself and triumphant. "I'd never do a thing like that. You know that. You know me better than that."

I smiled in return, but I was not quite so sure.

Chapter Three
Let It Be Done

The conversation had come to an end so much quicker and easier than I had imagined. No recriminations, explanations, tears, regrets, slamming of doors, packing of suitcases. All suspicions, hypotheses, doubts were put to rest in a single moment. I felt like a yacht on a windless day or a searcher who comes to the edge of a cliff and has no further path to take. What now? Back to normal? Back to routine? Back to habitual living? But what does that mean? I no longer knew. Again, I needed time to think.

As soon as Andrew left for his luncheon, I started to take a closer look at my life and what I was doing. I could see my existence as if from a distance, uninvolved and impartial. I clearly saw how empty my days had been—keeping house, entertaining clients, making my life so much part of Andrew's that I no longer could find my own path, my own way, my own career. Somehow the weeks had slipped by and I had never started anything significant—no new project, no further education, no charity work, because always there was the next function to attend or the next house guest to entertain.

The more I contemplated my situation, the more disenchanted I became. I had no purpose in life except the support of Andrew's career and even that seemed now quite meaningless in the scheme of world events and human progression. I could see myself now, wrinkled and old, looking back at my life and at what I had achieved, or rather what I had failed to achieve, and seeing only dark expanses of nothingness.

On the other hand, I thought back to my time at the Human Development Center and realized that however brief that interlude had been, it was important to my life and future and that I had been given such a unique opportunity for a purpose. I could not squander it now; I needed to grow the seeds that had been planted and find ways to multiply the knowledge I had received and pass it on to others. It made me think of the story of the talents and I reached for the New Testament of the Bible in search of its meaning:

"For it will be as when a man going on a journey called his servants and entrusted to them his property; to one he gave five talents, to another two, to another one, to each according to his ability. Then he went away. He who had received the five talents went at once and traded with them; and he made five talents more. So also, he who had the two talents made two talents more. But he who had received the one talent went and dug in the ground and hid his master's money.

"Now after a long time the master of those servants came and settled accounts with them. And he who had received the five talents came forward, bringing five talents more, saying, 'Master, you delivered to me five talents; here I have made five talents more.' His master said to him, 'Well done, good and faithful servant; you have been faithful over a little, I will set you over much; enter into the joy of your master.' And he also who had the two talents came forward, saying, 'Master, you delivered to me two talents; here I have made two talents more.' His master said to him, 'Well done, good and faithful servant; you have been faithful over a little, I will set you over much; enter into the joy of your master.' He also who had received the one talent came forward, saying, 'Master, I knew you to be a hard man, reaping where you did not sow, and gathering where you did not winnow; so I was afraid, and I went and hid your talent in the ground. Here you have what is yours.' But his master answered him, 'You wicked and slothful servant! You knew that I reap where I have not sowed, and gather where I have not winnowed? Then you ought to have invested my money with the bankers, and at my coming I should have received what was my own with interest. So take the talent from him, and give it to him who has the ten talents. For to every one who has will more be given, and he will have an abundance; but from him who has not, even what he has

*will be taken away. And cast the worthless servant into the outer darkness;
there men will weep and gnash their teeth."* (Matthew 25*)

Well yes, I had talents and I also believed that all people on Earth had
their own unique talents as well, which only they could offer to the
world and to others. At this stage I did not know exactly what these
talents were, but I had an inkling that they were to do with teaching
and healing and helping others. I felt privileged and marked by the
fact that I had been chosen to undergo such a unique education and
I knew at that moment that it was not meant for me alone. I needed
to find those who would listen and share with me my experiences
and lessons. I felt the weight of responsibility, that by accepting the
mysterious teachings I had received, I had now taken on the tasking
of passing them on to others where they might bear fruit and bring
positive results for the future of the human race.

"That's my story in a nutshell. That's where I am now." I was at
Anne's house, going through the whole story in detail, though I
omitted to mention that I had suspected her of being involved in an
affair with Andrew. It felt as if I was dispatching the events of the
past week so that I could move on. She sat very still and quiet, as if
waiting for me to continue.

"My life is about to change. From being a student I need to
become a teacher. I want to find the people who believe that life has
a meaning and that we are here to learn and grow. I now know that
material possessions are only important in that they allow a person
to do what they feel they need to do. The unseen commodities of
serenity and patience and care are so much more valuable, in that
they can transcend physical death."

I caught Anne's eye, and added, "Yes, I have changed. My entire
outlook on life has changed. I believe that beauty lives on the inside
and that each person forges their own destiny. Mine begins from here
and I can no longer be just another suburban housewife, for I see the
need for understanding, tolerance and compassion. I must pass my

---

** The Holy Bible, Revised Standard Version
The Catholic Truth Society, London, 1966*

test and earn my further training. And the only way I can do that is to undertake a journey to find those who need these lessons."

I fell silent for a moment. Anne responded at last.

"Before you make any dramatic changes, why don't we drive out to the Human Development Center and check it out? Otherwise, if it was all a dream, for example, you might be throwing away your entire life for nothing.

"All right. Let's go."

We drove out of town together, following the main road, checking the map as we went and looking for the small side road that would lead us to the school. We missed it the first time we attempted to find it and found ourselves driving out of the area altogether. We turned around and returned to the side road which we felt could be the one we were looking for. It seemed so different now—in broad daylight, with no mist hanging over the trees lining the road. It seemed wider and more accessible and we could plainly see the fields and farmhouses beyond the trees. The road also seemed smoother now and I no longer worried that two cars going in opposite directions might not be able to pass each other without almost coming to a halt.

The rise in elevation also seemed gentler and although there were small hills and a few bends, the good visibility ensured that there were no surprises lurking beyond these changes in the topography of the terrain. In fact, we had been driving at a fair pace for approximately twenty minutes and I began to worry that we had missed it. We could find nothing—no sign, no walled-in grounds, no large building with outbuildings and lawns in front of it. I remembered that I had first spotted the retreat center from the top of a hill; but this time there seemed to be no hill from which we could spot a likely view of the place. In fact, we seemed to be lost and I was quite sure we had missed it.

Another five minutes went by and I decided that we should turn around and go back. Anne was being skeptical, but she did not protest. She was now doubting whether I had ever really been there. Even I was beginning to question the testimony of my own memory and recollections.

"It was real, I tell you. It was just like talking to you today. I was there. I experienced all those lessons. Really."

In the meantime we had driven back to the main road and there was not a sign of the building or the gate or the driveway lined with trees. I began to wonder whether it had all been a dream.

"I give up. I don't know where it was. But it definitely was there," I said.

I turned back into the main road leading into town. At that very moment, I heard the Master's voice in my head, very distinctly saying, "You won't find it. You're not ready yet."

I said nothing to Anne, but simply remarked: "It's not there. You're right."

And we never mentioned it again.

Epilogue

Mostly people do not believe my story, but those who do will often ask me whether my life has changed since my experiences at the Human Development Center. I reply that yes, absolutely, it has changed completely. Perhaps not dramatically and perhaps not so much externally, but everything about me—how I think, what I want and what I do—is different.

I have learned that I am not separate from my environment and that I am here with a universal purpose to fulfill. It is up to me to find out what that might be but I know that it is certainly not for myself alone. I see myself now as a single cell in the multi-faceted complexity that the human race represents at this time. I believe that we live at a time of dramatic change and we can choose to be part of a new arising that will rewrite history and be the germination of a new era of fairness and advancement. Or we may choose to ignore all the signs and indications and prophecies and continue to be governed by the wish for easy gratification and greed.

In trying to find my way, I have been studying religion and philosophy, as well as art and human behavior. I have searched through the great works of literature and I have found many inspiring and uplifting stories and ideas to contemplate and wonder about. Nature has become my guide and my refuge and I look to the worlds of energy to find answers.

Above all, I am never alone because always in the background of my mind I feel part of this great and powerful universe and I believe and trust that there is an important part for me to play.

How exactly my future will unfold, I do not know. But I have become a student and observer of the natural worlds, wondering about the laws of nature and attempting to look at my surroundings with inquisitive eyes, always detecting what is new and freshly appearing within the environment—be it seasonal changes or any fresh sensations or feelings that might lead to new understanding.

I have come to realiize that change is my constant companion; in observing myself, I acknowledge and welcome the invitation to mature and grow. Every moment is an opportunity to learn and I am determined to be open to the many lessons that life daily confronts me with. So from this time on I have decided to look around me for guidance as to how best to proceed, because I believe that the Master is always there, waiting for the student to be ready.

www.ingramcontent.com/pod-product-compliance
Lightning Source LLC
Chambersburg PA
CBHW051832040426
42447CB00006B/495